Rationality and relativism

International Library of Sociology

Founded by Karl Mannheim

Editor: John Rex, University of Aston in Birmingham

Arbor Scientiae
Arbor Vitae
A catalogue of the books available in the **International Library of Sociology** and other series of Social Science books published by Routledge & Kegan Paul will be found at the end of this volume.

Rationality and relativism

In search of a philosophy and history of anthropology

I. C. Jarvie

Professor of Philosophy
York University, Toronto

Routledge & Kegan Paul
London, Boston, Melbourne and Henley

First published in 1984
by Routledge & Kegan Paul plc

14 Leicester Square, London WC2H 7PH

9 Park Street, Boston, Mass. 02108, USA

464 St Kilda Road, Melbourne,
Victoria 3004, Australia and

Broadway House, Newtown Road,
Henley-on-Thames, Oxon RG9 1EN, England

Set in Linotron Times 10/11 pt
by Input Typesetting Ltd, London
and printed in Great Britain
by Billing & Sons Ltd., Worcester

© I. C. Jarvie 1984

Library of Congress Cataloging in Publication Data

Jarvie, I. C. (Ian Charles), 1937–

Rationality and relativism.
(International library of sociology)
Bibliography: p.
Includes index.
1. Anthropology—Philosophy. 2. Anthropology—History.
I. Title. II. Series.
GN33.J358 1984   306'.01   83–27055

British CIP data available
ISBN 0–7102–0078–1

Contents

It is useful to know something of the manners of other peoples in order to judge more impartially of our own, and not despise and ridicule whatever differs from them, like men who have never been outside their native country. But those who travel too long end by being strangers in their own homes, and those who study too curiously . . . are ignorant of what is done among ourselves . . .

Descartes

Preface

Every academic subject has a past history and a present structure. In the present there are boundaries beyond which lie other disciplines, straddling the boundaries are borderline cases. Anthropology interfaces with sociology, biology, linguistics. Borderline hybrids include archaeology, ethno-musicology and primitive art. These boundaries are part of what we might call the intellectual structure of the subject. This is constituted by the central ideas, the polarizing issues, the lines of debate, the division into subfields, the contested ground, the divisions over methodology, philosophy, alliance, boundaries, and so on.

A subject's history consists in a debate with and about the past of the subject. Stocking (1968) has presented it as a choice between presentism and historism. Presentism asks of the past, how did we get to the present? Historism asks of the past, what really happened back then? As Stocking well knows, history emerges from the interaction of both questions. The historist issue of what debates truly animated the split in the Anthropological Society of London (Stocking 1971) is of interest to anthropologists as opposed to historians of intellectual societies because the issues are firmly located within the boundaries of anthropology's *present* self-definition. Present concerns alert us to certain historical questions. In exploring the past, their concerns make us reflect anew on our concerns as well as on how the subject moved from those (then) to these (now).

From my first contact with it I have found the subject of anthropology absorbing but incoherent. Incoherent because there seemed to be no discernible structure to the field. Academically it had its connections to archaeology and biology, and was split also into cultural and social. Students were discouraged from reading classics such as Frazer's *The Golden Bough* (1890) or

Boas's *The Mind of Primitive Man* (1911) as they were misleading about present concerns: a presentist injunction. They were encouraged to read Robertson Smith and Durkheim because they were precursors: another presentist sentiment. There was very heavy emphasis on technical mastery of kinship, politics and law, little attention to religious cosmology, child upbringing or art. Most puzzling of all was a sort of embargo on history, both of the peoples and customs being studied and the people and customs of anthropology itself. Apart from the few precursors, British students were taught that the subject had emerged fully developed from the brows of Bronislaw Malinowski and A. R. Radcliffe-Brown sometime around 1920 (Jarvie 1964b; Kuper 1973; Langham 1981).

My sense that this was an incoherent field was heightened by contact with American anthropology, where founding fathers, precursors, academic alliances and intellectual preoccupations were all somewhat different. Even anthropologists have imperialist tendencies in academic matters and the differences were the subject of strident trans-Atlantic polemic (Murdock 1951, Firth 1951, Eggan 1954).

Looking back now I see that a persisting intellectual quest has been to render this incoherent field coherent. The route I chose involved seeking out the intellectual ideas that animate both historical and present concerns and which provide continuity to the one and unity to the other. *The Revolution in Anthropology* (1964) was partly an attempt to explain what that revolution was and how it came about, and partly a plea for a more open-minded attitude to the achievements of predecessors and in presently pursued practice. It seemed to me that anthropology historically and correctly revolved around answers to problems about the nature, development and unity of mankind; problems that were both philosophical and scientific. I diagnosed a grievous scientism at work in Malinowski and Radcliffe-Brown that was opposed to facing these philosophical continuities and which instead tried to unify the field by professionalizing its practice (fieldwork).

This effort of mine was strongly resisted for many reasons, of which the most intriguing was one I trace to an empiricist allergy to ideas. Anthropologists agreed among themselves that the practices of the peoples they studied were to be explained not by animating ideas but by structural patterns and functional outcomes. So rain dances were said not to be satisfactorily explained by people's belief that such dancing would bring about rain. On the contrary, the dancers knew that rain did not come in the dry season but only in the wet, hence they stored food against drought and generally were not bamboozled about what causes what and how to survive in the physical world. But in a time of drought a rain dance articulated concern, drew the group together, facilitated mutual support and help, and integrated the present with the past. My summary of this kind of customary explanation was, 'study the ritual, not the belief'. Anthropologists ridiculed explanations using ideas by calling them if-I-were-a-horse arguments (Gluckman 1965). The man confronted with an escaped horse stands in front of the corral and thinks, 'if I were a horse where would I head?' This is supposed to be such an absurd procedure on the face of it that we will dismiss such reasoning out of hand. Since we can't be horses in our imagination we should search using scientific, geographical methods. Similarly with rain dances, we should abandon any attempt to get the savage point of view and look to the social context to explain what happens. If faced with the conundrum that explicating an action's functional consequences does not explain it, the philosophical reply was made that anthropology describes rather than explains.

A striking application of this line of thought was an antidote to the use of historical arguments to explain current practice. Faced with matrilineal societies (that they mistakenly called matriarchal), earlier protoanthropologists were said to have conjectured earlier states (e.g. 'primitive promiscuity') from which matriliny had emerged and from which in turn patriliny would emerge. Such if-we-were-primitively-promiscuous arguments were held not to explain because of a want of evidence that there ever were such prior states of affairs and also because they were intellectualist. That is to say, they postulated intellectual problems for the promiscuous (whose child is whose, etc.) that supposedly explain the decay of the system. But matriliny was stable, not decaying, as a form of social life rather than as intellectual construct. It was a way people acted or behaved, not a way people *thought*. And to this the more philosophically inclined could add a bit of philosophy: historical explanation without causal theory commits the fallacy of *post hoc ergo propter hoc*.

As in the history of mankind, so, it seemed, in the history of anthropology, what is going on now is not able to be explained by what previously happened. Fieldwork, theorising, teaching are going on now as part of a functioning academic subject. To explain its coherence it is sufficient to master how it works, how it is done.

To this position I produced the counter-example of Melanesian cargo cults, religious movements that were spread across many subcultures and social structures, disruptive and dysfunctional in many ways, and hence not amenable to explanation by structural pattern and functional outcome. In the end, I maintained, they could only be explained by an intellectualist account of culture clash. From beyond the cultural horizon of Melanesia had come peoples (the colonizers) bearing powerful sets of idea which they aggressively introduced into these societies taking little thought for the consequences. Whether or not the locals admired the whites at first, they soon found the system of wage-labour and colonialism oppressive. Yet they were offered a package consisting of material goods and an explanatory and legitimating body of ideas (education and missionary activities were fused). But even those who eagerly bought the ideas got few material goods and none of the power that went with them. That new explanations of this situation should be indigenously generated, fusing elements of imported ideas, with elements of local ideas, and that these explanations should manifest themselves as millenarian religious cults hardly seemed surprising. Confusion and disappointment were meliorated by a combination of thought and action.

By extension, I reasoned, thought can make sense of the incoherence of anthropology, and this thought would be philosophical and historical. Anthropological ritual behaviour might be a mutually reinforcing system, but neither its present shape nor its ultimate point could be discovered by that method of approach. So I determined, in both cargo cults and anthropology, to study the belief as well as the ritual. In a social science this means study the theoretical, philosophical and methodological ideas of the practitioners both at present and in the past. One can then trace back the branch of anthropology into the trunk of the tree of knowledge that goes back as far as the Greeks, who discovered and set many of the underlying problems. The historical problem of accounting for the succession of ideas since then can be treated intellectually as solving problems by proposing theoretical explanations, debating and testing them. This gives a slightly too neat rational reconstruction of the history of the subject from which pure historians can take off to discover the true dead-ends, detours and by-ways that actually constitute the history.

The present book focusses only on two points: the philosophical enterprise of anthropology and its depredation by the philosophy of relativism.

One consequence of an historical and philosophical exploration of anthropology is embarrassment. Not just because of factual error and sheerest speculation in our past, but because of the espousal of ideas we now find repugnant. I have in mind particularly one or other form of racialism. So embarrassing is this idea to present-day anthropology that it is a topic glossed over in many textbooks and treated highly polemically in others. That our intellectual ancestors were animated by racialism is to me an interesting fact that should be faced and explored fully and without embarrassment. Buried in it are animating ideas the refutation or modification of which give rise to anthropological ideas as we find them today. This is no blot on them. Furthermore, neither can our embarrassment be eased nor can a proper understanding of what if anything is mistaken about racialism be achieved without close and unembarrassed study of it.

Embarrassment at racialism and its consequences of genocide, slavery and discrimination is I believe behind the all-too-eager embracing of relativism in the profession. In the course of this monograph I shall try to show that relativism is intellectually disastrous because it is no barrier to racialism and it fosters intellectual attitudes from which anthropology still suffers. These include sloppy disregard of contradictions (especially between rationality and relativism), and abdication from the classical aim of the social sciences to enlighten, and improve the lot of, mankind.

Acknowledgments

Research for this volume was carried out with the help of a Nuffield Fellowship and an SSHRC Leave Fellowship both of which supplemented sabbatical leave from York University. An intellectual debt is owed to Richard Popkin who, in a talk in the early 1970s, first suggested the line of approach to the history and hence philosophy of anthropology I have pursued here. Some of the ideas here were tried out on audiences at the London School of Economics, Dartmouth College, McGill University, the University of Southern California and the University of Lethbridge.

I.C.J.
Santa Monica

Prologue

Metaphysical anthropology

But howe the people first began
In what contrey, or whens they cam,
For clerkes it is a questyon

John Rastell
Interlude of the Four Elements
(1520)

P.1 The fundamental problems of anthropology

The three fundamental problems of anthropology are: the problem of rationality, the problem of relativism, and the problem of the relation of rationality to relativism.

The problem of rationality is this: how can we sustain the principle of the rational unity of mankind in the face of the vast diversity of mankind's works and achievements, especially of culture, society and cognition?

The problem of relativism is this: how can we sustain the principle of the moral unity of mankind against the vast diversity of expressed views and practices on moral matters that we find amongst mankind?

The problem of the relation of rationality to relativism is this: how can we reconcile the principle of the rational unity of mankind with the principle of the moral unity of mankind?

All the particular problems of anthropology, I believe, can easily be shown to be versions or sub-problems of these three basic ones. They are, as formulated, philosophical problems or, to be more precise, metaphysical problems. This may incline those anthropologists who are still of a strenuously empiricist and hence anti-metaphysical persuasion to deny that they are at all concerned with such problems. I shall have more to say about this below. Suffice it here to say that it can be shown that metaphysical issues underpin most if not all scientific work.

Part of the work of philosophy consists of clarifying the problems as a preliminary to solving (or dissolving) them. This work of clarification can lead to the discovery that a putative problem is a pseudo-problem or merely a verbal problem. It is then appropriate to dissolve it. But genuine problems will survive

3

and benefit from reformulation. Hence I want to press further this effort to state these three problems.

To begin with, the problem of rationality. What is the principle of the rational unity of mankind, and why should we want to sustain it? If we ask what makes men men rather than beasts there are various plausible answers: language, culture, a large brain, the ability to use tools. Each of these is a particular version of the most venerable answer in western philosophy: what makes man unique is rationality, the capacity to apply reason to tasks. Mankind is a unity because of shared rationality. Regardless of whether rationality is construed as an inner capacity or as a feature of patterns of displayed behaviour, it takes little thought to see that not all humans are equal in regard to it. Some behave quite, as we say, irrationally. Others almost too rationally. It looks as though rationality is unevenly distributed. The best face we can put on this inequality is to make rationality a methodological principle: assume men are rational unless there is compelling evidence to the contrary. The problem then is how can this principle be sustained in the face of the bewildering degrees to which rationality is displayed or not displayed in human social life? This challenge has pushed anthropologists to explain complex kinship systems, leaderless groups, feuding and warfare, prescriptive and proscriptive marriage rules, taboos, witchcraft, mutilation and infanticide as diverse manifestations of the capacity to apply reason to tasks.

Now the problem of relativism. Some humans are moral giants, others are moral dwarfs. Perhaps the same is true of cultures. There are noble savages, barbarian savages. The principle of the moral unity of mankind is not the idea that all men live by the same morality, still less that they all live up to it to equal degrees. Rather is it the methodological decision to treat men as morally equal *in the first instance* (perhaps out of respect for their rationality). We extend them equal moral consideration for no other reason than that they are fellow human beings. But, there are at large in the world varying moral codes, most of which do not include the idea that all men should be presumptively treated as moral equals. The religious do not have that view of sinners, nor does Jew of Gentile, Christian of heathen, Muslim of infidel, Nuer of Dinka. On the contrary, the notion that one's own group is a (if not *the*) moral elect is far more common. How then is the anthropologist to sustain his belief in the principle of the moral unity of mankind in face of such countervailing principles? By research that minimizes the differences; by espousing the doctrine that morality is culturally relative and differences are to be expected; by contending that at a deeper level there is agreement.

Such ad hoc apologetic devices are too easy to use, and little of value has emerged from relativistic anthropological research.

And finally, the problem of the relation of rationality to relativism. Are the two principles consistent with each other? Is it rational to adopt the principle of moral unity; is it moral to adopt the principle of rational unity? This is tricky because most tribes deny both the rational and the moral unity of mankind. The tribe of anthropologists sets itself apart by its espousal of either. Yet as a tribe it feels it is inconsistent to set itself in judgment over the rest of humanity. Perhaps, they reason, the two principles are not inconsistent. Applying reason to tasks will produce differing moralities hence the principle of the rational unity of mankind entails moral relativism. This is inconsistent with the views of the tribes they study and sets them up in judgment *malgré leurs*. Starting reasoning from the principle of relativism leads to endorsing anti-rational unity ideas in the tribes they study—which are often elitist and racialist. Again, these confusions have produced inconclusive research.

In my view, the attribution of equal rational capacity should entail the attribution of equal moral responsibility; and the attribution of moral equality implies equal rational capacity. Why? Well, if, prima facie, people are equally capable of rational action then they are equally responsible for their actions; if we are to attribute to them equal moral responsibility we must also assume they have the rational capacity to use it. So these principles can be made consistent. Research in clear acknowledgment of them will be more fruitful.

P.2 The methodology of problems

In this work the word 'problem' is a technical one. It is perhaps the least appreciated aspect of Popper's philosophy of science that it places primary emphasis on problems. Only those who have studied with him seem fully appraised of the centrality of problems and the methodological fruitfulness of pausing over their formulation. Among recent philosophers of science, both Hattiangadi and Laudan have published work on the central role of problems, the former deriving his ideas from Popper and extending them, the latter going his own way. Unable to pin down Laudan's ideas (Jarvie, 1979) and hence to explain my assent and dissent crisply, I here concentrate on Popper and Hattiangadi.

Popper describes a problem as a breach in our horizon of expectations. Our horizon of expectations is the set of anticipations generated by our stock of current knowledge. Our current knowledge includes the science we know, the commonsense we have absorbed, and the information we have about the state of the world. This horizon includes mundane expectations such as that a metal chair will support our weight or that parents bring up children, and sophisticated ideas about the behaviour of elementary particles in accelerators or that end-of-the-world religious cults will disintegrate upon the failure of the world to end on schedule. A breach in the horizon is a disappointed expectation.

If a chair collapses when we sit on it we suspect it is faulty, we do not immediately question our assumption that metal can support our weight. Were we to find no defect this breach in our horizon might lead us to suspect our theories of the strength of metal. Such a move is not far-fetched and in fact led to the isolation of a new phenomenon called 'metal fatigue'. Anthropologists' horizons were breached when they came across societies in which children were raised by grandparents or by uncles, not by parents. They considered the possibility that these peoples were promiscuous and did not know which child belonged to whom. But the patterns of rearing were systematic, not confused or random, and, moreover, it turned out that no one was confused about who was the parent of whom. Eventually anthropologists were compelled to revise their horizon of expectations: child-rearing is not in all societies the exclusive provenance of parents. Workable social systems exist where uncles or grandparents do it.

If the particles in the bubble-chamber photograph deviate from expected paths physicists may put it down to a blip or an artefact of the machine. But if the deviation persists they revise their calculations or even their catalogue of particles. If an end-of-the-world cult manages to continue after a predicted Armageddon,[1] revisions may be needed in the ideas that led us to expect the cult to collapse, revisions perhaps in the simple-minded view that what binds cultists together is belief in the end-of-the-world rather than the embedding of that belief in a network of economic, kinship and political ties with other people. (Festinger et al. 1956; Jarvie 1981). Also a revision of the idea that the only possible response to a breach in the horizon is a revision of it, rather than an *ad hoc* repair (Evans-Pritchard 1937), again, sanctioned and reinforced by the social ties that embed and transcend the cult belief.

We can consider that the horizon of expectations resembles a set of statements of our ideas which, together with the information we have about the world, generates further statements, predictions. Sometimes what actually happens contradicts those predictions. Elementary logic leads us to conclude that of two contradictory statements, at least one is false. So we begin to search for the false. This is the basic logical structure of problem-methodology.

Hattiangadi continues the analysis by discussing the development of those connected clusters of ideas and research we think of as academic subjects and their sub-fields. His idea is that in response to certain problems there will arise competing ideas that are debated, possibly because they draw on deeply different – say metaphysical – sources. The problem will thus stand as a node in a line of debate from which new lines of debate will branch out, pursuing the problematics of each of the competing ideas. The simplest such case will be where debate is between two sides. There is nothing impossible about there being more candidates than two, it simply complicates the picture (Hattiangadi 1978/9 and 1983).

These methodological ideas are at work in the foundations of this monograph. It will be my claim that the deepest problem embedded in anthropology is what philosophers call the one and the many. This problem is not specific to the study of man; on the contrary, its appearance there is merely one manifestation. Perhaps its most general formulation is: is the world just one thing or many different things? Is there one basic substance or many? Parmenides was the great exponent of the universe as an undifferentiated unity. Democritus, the founder of atomism, suggested how the combination and arrangement of atoms of the basic substance could account for the variety in the world. Anthropologists are engaged in answering the problem of the one and the many applied to humankind. Is there one human race, or more than one? Is the diversity of man an appearance to be explained away or a reality that does the explaining?

The problem of the one and the many gives rise to two debating lines within anthropology: those exploring the line that mankind is indeed one and hence which try to account for human diversity; and those exploring the idea that mankind is diverse and which hence search for explanations of human unity. Each problem can be tackled in two ways: origin and structure. When pursued from the point of view of origin, the controversy is called that between polygeny (multiple origins) and monogeny (single origins). When pursued at the level of structure, the controversy is that between pluralism (many forms) and monism (one form). It is my contention that anthropology is the subject generated by the tension between the lines of debate that grow out of these contested positions. Rationality comes to explain the unity of mankind despite diverse appearances; relativism comes to explain the moral unity of mankind despite diverse appearances. Then the central issue becomes how to reconcile rational and moral unity . . .

P.3 Sketchy metaphysical history

A striking feature of British social anthropology in the 1950s was its being a subject without a history. Ancestors were acknowledged, of course, Morgan, Maine, Robertson Smith, Durkheim were the most frequently invoked, but they were treated as pre-scientists who had at best pointed the way to ideas now fully and scientifically developed.[2] Ancestor-worship and hence close study and application of their ideas was decidedly not encouraged. This view, that historical study is controlled by the search for the ancestry of current ideas, is known as presentism; the concerns of the present control historical research and writing.[3] Opposed to presentism is historism, the view that history is an attempt to find out how things seemed at the time, and how present concerns emerged from that background; historical research and writing are controlled by and hence turn to the historical past (Stocking 1968). Lowie's *History of Ethnological Theory*, Tax's *From Lafitau to Radcliffe-Brown*, White's *The Social Organization of Ethnological Theory*, Eggan's *One Hundred Years of Anthropology* are all, to one extent or another, presentist travesties of what might recklessly be called the real history of anthropology. This would be true even of the historical asides in Evans-Pritchard's *Social Anthropology*, and is especially obvious in his scornful *Theories of Primitive Religion* – which reads like that theologians used to call 'A Catalogue of Errors'. Margart Hodgen, George Stocking and J. W. Burrow made valiant pioneer attempts to write the history of anthropology as it really happened. In this they have not always been followed.[4]

A serious history is not just one that goes back to primary documents but one which also, in intellectual history at least, takes ideas seriously. This involves thinking through the systems of ideas of different periods; ideas we may find bizarre, superstitious and even embarrassing, but which nevertheless may underlie developments that lead to our present concerns. Confining attention solely to the post-medieval period, the broad intellectual question I want to answer is how the transition came about from philosophical anthropology in the seventeenth and eighteenth centuries to social anthropology in the twentieth; how we get from the monogenism/polygenism controversy of the seventeenth century to the present; how we get from the evolution/diffusion debate of the turn of the century to the present: how we get from a transatlantic community of anthropological thought in the eighteenth and nineteenth centuries to the separation of (British) social anthropology and (American) cultural anthropology in the twentieth. (And why did British social anthropology develop in the particular way it did?)

I haven't worked out answers to all these questions, but I will share what I have. Alarmingly, for those who want anthropology to be an empirical science, the answers seem to lie in the meta-physical underlay of scientific research, and debates about meta-physics punctuate the history of physics[5] so it is not here being used as a dirty word. Indeed it is usually the only clue to why a subject drifts the way it does. Trying to reconstruct the meta-physical history of anthropology is like trying to do the Jackson Pollock jigsaw puzzle. Jackson Pollock was the American painter of the post-war period who painted by dribbling and smearing paint on canvas. Faced with a randomly selected array of jig-saw pieces, of closely similar shape and colour, one tries to piece them together unsure whether the result will be a discernible pattern. Unlike the jig-saw puzzle, the history of anthropology is the result of human action but not of human design: that there is a *correct* arrangement of the parts, that it is clear what is a part and what is not, is by no means guaranteed. History is the explanatory reconstruction of the past not the recapturing of it.

This viewpoint forces the historian to conjecture patterns and connections and to test them for explanatory power, logical consistency and empirical character. We can call this rational reconstruction. It proceeds as follows. Assume first that there is history, i.e. there is something to be explained. This then allows some tentative selection to be made as to what is and what is not part of that history. Such assumptions and their associated selec-tion principles will be of a very general, metaphysical character. To change the metaphor, metaphysics is the gross anatomy of the history of anthropology, or *a* possible gross anatomy.

My fundamental contention will be that all anthropological acti-vity, whether Hebrew, Greek, Roman, medieval, rationalist, philosophical, enlightenment, evolutionist, diffusionist, racialist or environmentalist, polygenist, monogenist, speculative or empir-ical, cultural or social, functionalist or structuralist, theoretical or empirical, consists fundamentally in meditations upon the problem of the unity of mankind. What, however, is the problem of the unity of mankind? I speculate that the doctrine of the unity of mankind was a bold conjecture put forward by some thinker – let us call him a philosopher – who refused to be impressed by the diversity or dissarray among men, by the ethnocentrism if not racialism manifested by most groups towards other groups, and who dismissed all of it as deceptive appearance concealing under-lying reality or unity. Who this bold and perhaps foolhardy genius was, we shall never know. Nor need we know. We do know that Pericles of Athens, whether sincerely or not, gave a clear crystallization of the doctrine in a document of fifth-century Athens.

For what it is worth, I suggest that the primal condition of man *qua* anthropologist was as a member of a band of hunters and gatherers roaming a territory. And that this territory was the boundaries of his universe, touched here and there by contacts, some friendly, some hostile, with other bands. When this creature, this proto-anthropologist, confronts through trade, migration or whatever, a totally different language, culture and society, his first hypothesis is that the human beings (as nearly all groups call themselves) have come across some strange new creature, similar to but different from themselves, like us but not quite one of us. Defensively, he defines mankind, the human beings, as his own group.

Such ethnocentrism becomes more difficult to maintain when there is contact with a group that is admired: this, I conjecture, could come about in trade or war. A group makes an object, or tool, grows a crop or mines an element that is much admired or coveted by other groups; a group fights and dominates others. Logically, it would be possible for a group to de-value itself in relation to those admired others. But I am intrigued by the thought that transcends particular differences and says we are all one family.

What arguments could be used to minimize the differences? Obviously, stress on the similarities. We are all born and die; people from different groups can have children by one another; we all need food, water, sleep and salt; we differ more from stones and other animals than we do from each other; we can learn from one another.

Notice the metaphysical boldness of such arguments: diversity is appearance; unity is reality. Notice also that the doctrine has immediate physical and ethical corollaries. Men and women of different appearance can interbreed, but men and horses cannot. If we are all members of one family, then we should act towards one another as we do in the family. It is interesting how opponents of the unity of mankind, as late as the American racialist Lothrop Stoddard writing in the 1920s and 1930s, deny both consequences.[6] They say many miscegenate unions are infertile and that mulattoes are a sickly lot who cannot themselves breed very well; and they see no reason why those of different race shouldn't be treated differently, i.e. unequally.

For those persuaded of the unity of mankind the principal problem is to explain its contradiction by the immense physical, cultural and social diversity manifested by mankind. How did this diversity come about? For the polygenists the principal problem is to explain the evidence of unity, especially man's capacity to interbreed, communicate, trade, in a way he can with no other animal. The metaphysics of unity sires an anthropology that explains diversity; the metaphysics of diversity sires an anthropology that explains unity. Anthropology starts from the hoary old problem of the one and the many.

It is interesting that the Old Testament contains a complex anthropology speaking to these problems. It can be read as starting from unity since all mankind descends from Adam. Various events and catastrophes disperse and differentiate men, but there is only one God, one truth, one species of men. Yet the text will yield other readings. There are passages in several stories that remind the anthropologist of tribalists proclaiming their God is the only one *for them*, leaving open the question of what is good for others. The most ingenious polygenist reading is due to a mysterious seventeenth-century thinker called Isaac de la Péyrère, to whom we shall come presently.

Greek anthropology similarly will yield both strands of thought. Deterioration from a Golden Age, and Greek elitism, were better at exploring the savage/civilized problem, which is a special case of diversity, than with coping with the general problem of diversity in unity. It is not my intention to do a history of anthropological thought. I want now to make a jump to 1492 and then to 1655, because I think both years saw radical new departures in the unity/diversity debate. 1492 saw the 'discovery' (O'Gorman 1961) of America and the disclosure of the presence there of – well, of what? Of men? Of men-like creatures? In the end the notion of savagism as a stage on the road to civilization was invented as a category to fit the American aboriginal population (Pearce 1953). Men, yes; not barbarous; potentially civilized; potential Christians. But whence came they?

All men were descended, so the Bible insisted, from Noah and Adam. How did these descendants get from the Middle East – to where was it? – Asia, the New World, America? How was it they had brought no recognizable version of Judaism with them (or perhaps they did: Thorowgood 1650–1660; L'Estrange 1662; Eliot 1660). A debate raged from about 1590 (Acosta) onwards, first in Spanish, then in Dutch and English, on this topic. Asia, Atlantis, Corinth, Ophir and the Lost Tribes were offered as origins for the Indians. One authority (García 1607) listed about twelve theories and affirmed them all. A later commentator (Barcia) added thirteen more and affirmed those as well. The strongest arguments were for a land crossing from Asia. The trouble was the elapse of time permitted by the Bible after the flood, dated

11

some 2000-odd BC, was hardly enough to account for the changes in and spread of mankind. This argument was used to great effect in what is known as the Pre-Adamite controversy, which Popkin sees as the philosophical origin of modern racialism (Popkin 1974a and b, 1978).

In 1655 a sensation was caused by a book called *Pre-Adamites* or *Men Before Adam* by one Isaac de la Péyrère. Grappling with the problems of cultural diversity, the origins of the Indians, and the Biblical stories and chronology, he cracked them all by expanding the time scale. Genesis, he concluded, was only the story of the Jews. The Gentiles, dispersed throughout the old and new worlds, were much older, products of a prior creation, descendents of an earlier but unnamed Adam.

His book was a best-seller, but was publicly burned by the authorities and he himself had a narrow escape from a similar fate. Some two dozen or more replies to it appeared in the space of a few years (Allen 1949). Nevertheless, La Péyrère had set the new terms of a debate that would continue from then onwards: he had burst certain constraints the ideas of the Bible had placed on men's thinking. Men as one species would not fit the Biblical chronology. Their physical and cultural diversity and their scattering over the face of the earth could not be accounted for by any known means if the world began in about 4000BC and if all creation was wiped out by the flood. Calculations showed it was impossible for the animals to have bred and repopulated the earth since Noah.

> The same negligence which possessed the first, pursued the successive Doctors of the Church; who knew no other men, but such as were begotten by *Adam*; Yea, they pronounced them Hereticks, that placed the *Antipodes* over against Adams posterity; because they must then think them the posterity of some body else. I would St. *Augustine* or Lactantius were now alive, who scoff'd at the *Antipodes*. Truly they would pity themselves, if they should hear or see those things which are discover'd in the East and West *Indies*, in this clear-sighted age, as also a great many other Countries full of men; to which it is certain none of *Adams* posterity ever arrived. (La Péyrère, 1655, p. 276)

La Péyrère's brilliance is that he took the bold, dangerous, but ultimately correct way out: he overthrew the Biblical chronology. He subjected Genesis and the Epistle to the Romans to close scrutiny and showed that law and sin are said to exist when Adam comes on the scene, that Cain is marked so that those who come across him, the fratricide, will not kill him, and he goes to the

East of Eden and founds a city. With whom and with tools from whence, Péyrère asks? How could he possibly be the sole surviving human being?

Others, less bold, are provoked to strenuous effort to give environmentalist accounts of how Adam's descendants could have crossed the oceans, differentiated themselves into blacks, browns, yellows, reds and whites, developed hundreds of different languages, religions, customs and social forms. It was a tall order. In fact it was quite impossible. But environmentalism seemed the only hope of reconciling the egalitarian metaphysics of the unity of mankind with the Bible.

The alternative was to conclude that men belonged to not one but several species, separately created in different parts of the world at different times. This line of thought also does not sit too well with the Bible unless the lemma is added that the Bible narrates the story of *mankind*, and that other men-like creatures are part of the animal kingdom, the creation of which is skipped over in the Bible. Hence, there is in the eighteenth century much discussion of the theory that negroes are related to orang-outangs. So: there are men, and there are men-like beasts; in sophisticated accounts there are intermediate groups called barbarians, primitives, savages, wild men, wild children, not totally anarchic, but rude and simple; sometimes with and sometimes without the potential to be brought into civilization depending on who is arguing. (Pearce 1953, Huddleston 1967, Jordan 1968, Sinclair 1977, Berkhofer 1978, Sheehan 1980)

Monogenism versus pluralism, nature versus nurture, evolution versus diffusion, all these controversies, which still continue, have their modern roots in these metaphysical-cum-factual disputes. We are tempted, of course, to see emancipationists as good Christian egalitarians and environmentalists, and pro-slavers, as racialist polygenists. But slavery is really a separate issue and is an unreliable predictor of the anthropological doctrines people will espouse.

Contemporary training in anthropology discourages discussion of these sorts of metaphysical and historical issues. The trouble with conjectural history according to Radcliffe-Brown (1952, p. 50) was not that it was history, but that it was conjectural. He was against speculation and for empirical observation and science; in William James's terms, so beloved of Herskovits (1951, p. 35), he was tough-minded rather than tender-minded. Indeed the sea-change which I have called 'The Revolution in Anthropology' (Jarvie 1964) was more than anything else an attempt to set anthropological debate on a solid grounding of empirical study. Like Radcliffe-Brown, I am in favour of science and of empirical

13

enquiry, but I hold that conjecture and speculation (and meta-physical speculation, at that) are a necessary and lasting part of the enterprise and to me at least the most interesting part.

Has the transformation of anthropology into an empirical science succeeded in solving the problems with which anthropology has been concerned since the Greeks? The answer could be predicted in advance. Because the underlying problems are metaphysical and moral, empirical data can at best verify the preselected view with which the anthropologist begins.

A rational reconstruction of the history of field studies or empirical anthropology might look like this. Believing that the manifest diversities of society and culture were founded on deep psychological and physical differences, racialists set out to map mankind. Egalitarians, convinced that diversity was superficial and was underlain by a basic unity and similarity also set out to map mankind. Two metaphysics, one result – fieldwork. How mistaken then, are those who claim that by fieldwork racialism and ethnocentrism are refuted and egalitarianism and relativism vindicated.

There are two little clouds on this neat horizon, one is that racialism is not just a dead doctrine like flat-earthism; its surviving adherents (all doctrines have their partisans) are *execrated*. Vitriolic controversies have surrounded the ideas of the physical anthropologist Carleton S. Coon, and the psychologist Arthur F. Jensen simply because they were suspected of saying things that racialists might exploit.[7] The other cloud is just this: both racialism (there exists deep down physical and psychological differences between men corresponding to differences in skin pigment), and egalitarianism (there exists deep down a physical and psychological unity of mankind despite differences of skin pigmentation) are metaphysical doctrines. As such, they can be confirmed by evidence, but they cannot be refuted by it.[8]

In this monograph I embrace neither the single origin nor the separate origins view of mankind. These are issues for specialists whose quarrels I prefer to look on. But I do plump for the unity of mankind. This is logically defensible by detaching it from issues of the biology and anthropology of the human race. The unity of mankind need not be a literal truth of descent for us to embrace it. It can be, instead, a programme: a proposal for how to act and think. We can act towards our fellow human beings with the same consideration and respect we would to family members, and we can set ourselves the task of exploring biology and anthropology under the control of that moral unity. Were it to transpire that human beings are of several families with somewhat different endowments, it would not follow that the programme of treating others as of equal value to ourselves should be abandoned. We adopt it for quite other reasons.

So, very quickly, anthropology as a fieldwork science can be seen to have a crucial moral and metaphysical underlay without which it cannot be understood, but to the solution of which it can provide no help. In *The Revolution in Anthropology* I tried to explain why endless doses of the facts of fieldwork are so boring. Because what the fieldwork involves is going to an exotic society and succeeding in making good sense to the outsider of its customs and institutions. So each monograph in effect says, 'Look here! Pretty bizarre, eh. Just what you expected of benighted, irrational, anarchic primitives. But now look closer. What do you see? They live an ordered, reasonable, perhaps even admirable social life.' The first and perhaps the second exposure to this strategy is revelatory. Subsequently, one balks because we already know that it is true, and repetition consists of preaching to the converted.

Egalitarianism and racialism have then the same source: the problem of diversity; one says it is illusory and the other that it is real. Both are the origins of anthropology since both seek out facts to confirm their prejudices and refute the other side. The facts should, actually, refute both the view that diversities are illusory and the view that they are a fixed reality. Mankind possesses both unity and diversity.

What is the problem of diversity? Men's manners, *mores*, values, social organizations, habits of thought and the like, differ widely over time and space. So wide are these differences that the naturalness, reasonableness, *normality*, of our own social practice is thrown into question. What is the significance of these differences, how do they square with a fundamental metaphysical and ethical commitment to the unity of mankind? Either, there is no unity any longer, or, it is the *claim* to unity that has to be explained and justified, rather than the diversity. This puts the egalitarian on the defensive against the racialist, woe to him.

Diversity is very deep. Not all the diverse adaptations man has made to his environment are equally effective, or flexible, and this ultimately is why I would claim that while diversity is real, yet for many purposes men should be treated as equal (egalitarianism) and diversities should not be regarded as fixed divisions (racialism).

So why did British social anthropology and American cultural anthropology cleave to and verify one solution to the problem of the unity of mankind namely that men are equal and diversities mere appearance? Perhaps we could cite the personalities of Boas, Malinowski and Radcliffe-Brown as together being a sort of Cleopatra's nose: had it not been for them things would have been

different. But why then did Radcliffe-Brown turn from the traditional anthropology of his teacher Rivers to Durkheim—to sociology, whose problem is not the unity of mankind, but, how is
social order possible? How is social order possible, surprisingly,
becomes a problem in the United States only after one hundred
years of being the first new nation (Lipset 1963). A Frenchman,
Alexis De Tocqueville, not Americans, wondered how society is
possible, how things can work without aristocracy and hierarchy.
The American case was problematic because there the attempt
was being made to create social unity from a population with great
diversity of origins and interests, dispersed over a vast territory.
In a traditional European society such as England the problem of
diversity did not arise except at the outposts of empire, where
crude ethnocentrism and racialism did need to be modified if the
colonizers were to be effective. Only by close-grained reflection
on similarities and differences with subject peoples was it possible
to govern them by that mixture of paternalism and indirect rule
that was the British Empire's speciality.[9] Is it an accident that so
many big names in British social anthropology were foreigners
or colonials? Malinowski (Poland), Gluckman, Schapera, Fortes
(South Africa), Firth (New Zealand), etc.? There is a connection,
I suggest, between the social and cultural marginality of anthropologists and their preferred solution to the problem of the unity of
mankind. The socially marginal or the outsider can legitimate his
own assimilation if unity is reality and diversity is appearance.
Participant observation is the fantasy of penetrating an alien
society without causing significant disturbance, and achieving
sufficient acceptance or assimilation to obtain substantial amounts
of information. How closely this parallels the outsider wanting to
have access to being an insider while yet preserving self-identity.
The ability of primitive societies to cope with intruding anthropologists, to absorb outsiders and immigrants, leads to the problem
of how social order is possible, how is it done?

British colonialism sought a structure, indirect rule, that
involved minimal interference with local custom and culture.
French colonialism offered direct bureaucratic rule through
assimilated locals. American internal colonialism offered either
assimilation (with prejudice) or separation (reservations); the
former respected neither culture nor structure; the latter respected
culture but not structure, because reservations had to conform
their structures of power to those of the United States, e.g. U.S.
Criminal law applied to reservation life, governing councils were
given strictly circumscribed local powers that could at all times be
overridden.

Perhaps the personalities and experiences of Boas, Sapir,

16

Kroeber, Linton, Redfield, Benedict and Mead can be tied to the theory and practice of American anthropology.

Cross-cutting ties are also discernible. Malinowski and Boas's emphasis on extended fieldwork and linguistic competence reflects perhaps the foreigner who immigrates. Radcliffe-Brown, Evans-Pritchard, Fortes, Gluckman, Schapera and Firth reflect the structure of the colonialist experience. Benedict with little fieldwork and strong experience of marginality may treat anthropology as culture shock (Mead 1974).

For all these reasons, as well as perhaps the impact of biology and antipathy to creationist polygenism, the weight of anthropological opinion in this century has been on the side of unity. Believing in the unity of mankind's rationality, anthropologists have sought for universal structural principles or cultural laws that govern social organization. Believing that those of the same species are equal in their moral standing, they have sought to find common principles in men's diverse moral systems. These lines of debate are not consciously pursued or well argued. So that it is not their metaphysical and philosophical character that is at fault. Rather is it that there is a tendency to argue by verification, as though more and more new material somehow strengthens the basic claim. Even so it strengthens two claims whose reconciliation is by no means a foregone conclusion: if men are rational how is it that they have reached such diametrically opposed positions in morality?

Part one

Rationality

1.1 The problem stated

In this part I want to pose and to solve the problem of rationality: namely, in what does the vaunted rationality of human beings consist? To do this I shall engage in further discussion of what the problem is and of other solutions offered to it. My own solution will be that rationality is our capacity to apply reason to tasks. This is done most efficiently when we apply reason to the task of applying reason to tasks, in other words, when we try to learn from experience how to get things done. On this view rationality comes down to the idea that man is the animal who both learns from experience, and learns how to learn from experience, and does both to a much higher degree than his neighbours on the evolutionary tree.

Clearly, individuals will vary in their capacity to learn from experience. That variation can be lessened or increased by their attitude. If they adopt the aim of learning, and the aim of learning about learning, differences due to capacity will be minimized. Further, if they pool their efforts, individual variations of capacity and attitude will become irrelevant. My argument will be that social institutions have among their functions assisting us to learn from experience. Some institutions, like language and the division of labour, seem to have emerged spontaneously; others, like schools and laws, were invented. The supreme embodiment of mankind's rationality, I shall argue, is the partly designed and fairly recent social institution of science. Here the application of reason to tasks, including the application of reason to the task of applying reason to tasks (methodology) has been carried furthest. Science has developed new and powerful languages such as mathematics and chemical formulae, new and powerful machines such as microscopes, telescopes, accelerators and computers, constantly to improve not only what we know, but also what we know about how we get to know.

This view has the power to explain and clarify the debates over the problem of rationality in anthropology, and also to avoid the inconsistencies other solutions to the problems get into.

As is clear from the above, behind the discussion of the rational unity of mankind there stands a very ancient and very interesting problem: namely, what demarcates men from beasts? If it weren't perfectly obvious that men and beasts are different in many ways, there is always the fact that they cannot interbreed, a fact which must be ancestrally ancient folk-knowledge. You can produce an ass but you cannot produce a centaur. And while, in some of its manifestations, the life man leads resembles in some ways that of animals, the mere fact that we are all living, moving, breathing, bleeding creatures does not disguise the sense that men are something very special in the animal kingdom.

1.2 Ideas about reason and rationality

Aristotle is usually credited with the idea that man can be characterized not by his two-leggedness, since many animals are that, nor by his featherlessness, for many animals are that, but by his reason, his rationality.[1] Man is the rational animal. Having said this, it would be a philosophical mistake of the first order to set off on a quest that asks what exactly this rationality consists in. The problem under consideration, we must constantly remind ourselves, is how to distinguish man from other animals. Man displays certain traits we call rational and which we cannot detect, or only vestigially, in other animals. Our collective name for these is 'reasoning' or 'rationality'. This consists of memory; of planning and organization; of deferring gratification; of ratiocination and calculation; of intelligible communication; of problem-solving.

Some anthropologists are inclined to focus not on the somewhat nebulous idea of reason but on what they consider its embodiment, namely language. To display memory, planning, gratification, ratiocination, intelligibility and problem-solving we need, it seems, language. *Man is the language-using animal.* This shifts the problem from that of demarcating man from other animals to that of demarcating proto- or pre-languages, such as the calls of animals, the dances of bees, systems of gesture and co-ordination, from what we may like to think of as the higher and qualitatively different language men use.

Formulated thus as the problem of the emergence of language,

22

demarcating men from beasts seems insoluble. Any attempt to specify a point where language begins will have precursors, hence borderline cases, hence no clear demarcation. This seems to be one reason why Chomsky and his followers reject an evolutionary approach to the emergence of language. Man the language-using animal has to emerge fully formed with his capacity to learn language in place.[2] Most anthropologists would not want their studies of the problem of demarcating united mankind from the rest of the animal kingdom to lead them to anti-evolutionist positions.

Other anthropologists generalize still further and argue that language is only one among many tools that men employ and create, and that no other animal does this in other than vestigial ways, and that the employment of tools in some way embodies the rationality of mankind. *Man is the tool-using animal*.

But, if other animals possess simulacra of language and of tools, however vestigial, the hope for a crisp demarcation between man and the other animals evaporates. The same goes for '*man is the culture-creating animal*' because vestigial language and vestigial tools yield vestigial culture. And if rationality is linked to brain size, the continuities with other animals are greater than the discontinuities. It is a question whether a crisp demarcation should be sought. In the post-Darwinian era we are as aware of the continuities in evolution as we are of the leaps and breaks. Man is not crisply different from his animal ancestors, and hence may not be sharply differentiable from them. Yet there are features of the behaviour of man, of his acquisition and use of tools including language, that yield a demarcation that is fairly crisp. As indicated, I would focus on the capacity to learn from experience, to store that learning and to recall and transmit it at will, and hence to learn about learning from experience. The human animal does not rely on blind evolution to give him the capacity to cope with his ecological niche. Rather he employs a two-pronged strategy: he adapts himself; and he attempts to modify the niche. Some of the processes involved may be anticipated in one or other of the lower orders of the animal kingdom. Other animals migrate, beavers build dams, some animals seek and remember good hunting, and so on. But the capacity of man not just to apply reason to tasks but to learn to improve his application of reason to tasks is unmatched.

So we might sum up with the notion that survival and thrival is the aim, and the rationality of the animal man consists in his unique capacity to articulate that aim and contemplate diverse and effective means of achieving it; applying reason to tasks. The resulting wonders we call man's works: his societies, cultures and civilizations. They embody the principle of learning from experience – not relying on instinct or programming, not continuing on as before, not merging aim and achievement, not proceeding blindly.

This is what applying reason to tasks amount to. Now the question arises about the rational unity of mankind. This is the doctrine that man is in effect a homogeneous animal each example of which is endowed with more or less the same capacity to learn from experience. One of the clearest expressions of this idea is at the start of the modern period in Bacon's *Novum Organum* (1620). He there allows that men may differ in their capacities but argues that relative to the enormous differences between men and animals, between the stupidest man and the cleverest animal, the differences between men are not worth bothering about: Methodology eliminates them.

> certainly, if any one were to undertake, by steadiness of hand and power of eye, to draw a straighter line, or a more perfect circle, than anyone else, he would be inducing a comparison of abilities; but if he were to assert that by applying a rule or compasses he could draw a straighter line, or a more perfect circle, than anyone else could by the help of eye and hand alone, he certainly would be no great boaster. Now this remark applies not only to this our first and initial attempt, but also to those who shall hereafter follow up this subject. For our method of discovering Sciences goes far to equalize men's abilities, and leaves them individually no great room for excelling, since it performs everything by most certain rules and demonstrations. (Bacon 1620, Book I, Aph. cxxii.)

Bacon, who is often taken to be the prophet of the modern scientific age, went on from this principle of the rational unity of mankind to propose a radical new method of learning from experience, in effect of being rational. He saw learning hitherto tied into existing social hierarchies, institutions, taboos, and traditions, and grievously inhibited by them. By denying their legitimacy as auspices for enquiry, i.e. by undermining the arguments that showed this or that class of persons, this or that tradition of thinking, in fact possessed merit; by arguing for similarity of capacity in most men, he prepared the way for his Great Instauration, which he conceived of as a new world built on the basis of a science to which many men, not just some special privileged few, could contribute. He suggested the task of learning from experience could be divided up into fields and parcelled out to research teams for rapid completion. Rationality is for Bacon a capacity given to all men and to actualize it they have to adopt a

radically critical attitude and create certain kinds of social organization. These are elements of my own view of rationality.[3]

While I find Bacon's enthusiasm and boldness charming, I do
not doubt for a moment that both his radicalism and his optimism
were naive. A radical break from the past is easier thought than
achieved; research is hard both to organize and to do, while
success is by no means guaranteed. All normal adult members of
mankind may indeed be endowed with a basic modicum of reason;
whether the differences in whatever extra capacity they have are
unimportant is highly doubtful; and whether other things about
them such as temperament and emotion will allow them to
exercise what capacity they have to the full is also doubtful. We
cannot ascribe a rational essence to man such that it is uniformly
distributed amongst all the members. Man may differentiate
himself from other animals by an extraordinary capacity to learn
from experience; many are the men, nevertheless, who cannot
and will not learn from experience.

1.3 Reduction of variation

Having given some idea of what sort of theory of rationality is
being advocated in this monograph, let us now use it to look
briefly at the ordinary employment and history of the term. (If
the reader wonders why we did not proceed inductively by surveying usage first the answer must be that there is no observation
without theory, explicit theory is better than implicit, and we look
to rectify the confusion of usage rather than the reverse.)

We use 'rationality' and its cognates 'rational', 'reasonable' and
'rationalism' in diverse ways, e.g. we speak of:

1 rational action
2 rational behaviour
3 rational belief
4 reasonable attitude
5 reason versus emotion
6 rational versus intuitive thought
7 rational modes of (social or industrial) organization
8 technological rationality
9 bureaucratic-legal rationality
10 Bertrand Russell was a life-long rationalist
11 Irrationalist philosophers like Hegel
12 Man's irrational nature

These are only a few of the welter of uses we make of the terms
that cluster around rationality. And in addition to straightforward
variations of meaning, these expressions sometimes carry an

emotional charge: we can use rationality and its cognates as hooray/boo words, to call someone or something rational is to commend it; to call someone irrational is almost to abuse them. There is also the reverse emotional overtone: rationality is sometimes taken to connote a life-denying, emotion-stifling attitude, conjuring up visions of cold-hearted science and monstrously destructive technology. This charge was levelled by the high priest of irrationalism, D. H. Lawrence, at the high priest of rationalism, Bertrand Russell. The latter claims nearly to have been destroyed by the attack.[4]

When Russell proclaimed himself a rationalist what did he mean? That he abhorred emotion? That he was against life? Certainly not. He meant rather that he believed that philosophy, or intellectual enquiry of any kind should be conducted in as simple, clear and unambiguous a way as possible. Questions should be clearly asked, and arguments clearly set out. Similarly, when British philosophers, who participate in the tradition that owes a great deal to this example of Russell, condemn continental philosophers like Hegel, Kierkegaard and Heidegger as 'irrationalists', they mean they find their writings unclear: vague, ambiguous, with scarcely discernible theses and arguments. The association of clarity with rationality comes about because it is hard to learn from experience if your learning process is cloudy and obscure. Indeed, in the face of vagueness and obscurity it is hard to say whether anything is being discussed, let alone whether learning is going on.

An overtone of Russell's rationalism was his opposition to all organized religion and all private superstition. A rejection of the supernatural. This again does not mean he was without religious sense. His pellucid introduction to philosophy, *The Problems of Philosophy* (1912) closes with passages anyone would identify as broadly 'religious' in sentiment.

> through the greatness of the universe which philosophy
> contemplates, the mind also is rendered great, and becomes
> capable of that union with the universe which constitutes its
> highest good. (Russell 1912, final words)

His fiercest opposition was to organized religion as it is embodied in so much doctrine and ritual, namely obscure, vague, ambiguous and at the same time pretentiously grandiose in its claims. He was inclined to dismiss it as fraud and humbug, if not positively evil. To those who defend its obscurantism and dogmatism the rationalist must argue that these are obstacles to learning from experience.

Before proceeding, some discussion of the samples of usage just listed is in order. 1–4 are already under lengthy discussion. 5, 6 and 12 are psychological and we will come to them presently. 10–11 we have explored briefly. Uses 7–9 come from sociology, and especially Max Weber from whom we have taken our theory of rationality as the application of reason to tasks. Weber's own theory was that action in pursuit of goals was rational. Shifting from the adjectival to the noun form we would get, 'rationality is just that pursuit of goals', and this is more cryptic than helpful since its lack of reflexivity inhibits the application of standards of rationality to the task of ranking both goals and their manner of pursuit. Rationality enjoins us to learn from experience and that includes reflexively learning about rationality.

Now we come to psychology: reason versus emotion, rational versus intuitive thought, man's irrational nature. These are usages that connote a number of images that we shall explore one by one. To begin with a general point.

When psychologists label behaviour 'irrational' they mean something like not congruent with reality, not based on learning from experience. Fantasies, fears, guilts and so on are mental constructions that can become fixed and immune to the checks of experience. This is psychosis. Hence the psychotic person in acting to achieve what he wants, applying reason to tasks, persistently fails and displays what we call neurotic and psychotic patterns of behaviour which, on some level, are certainly very far from what he or she wants. (Which is not to rule out the possibility that at another level the person may be aware of the neurotic or psychotic behaviour as an option that he or she selects because it enables him or her to cope with the problems of the world.)[5]

Both psychologists and anthropologists were for long advocates of the idea that man had what they called an 'irrational side' to something else they called his 'nature', or 'human nature'. The model was that of a split mind – one side rational, cool, calculating, detached; the other side warm, feeling, impulsive, involved; the conflict was captured in the contrast of reason versus emotion. Moreover, even a rationalist philosopher such as David Hume believed that emotion – the passions – was the stronger and deeper of the sides to man's nature. Reason had constantly to struggle out into the light, and even so would always remain the 'slave' of the passions.[6] Why this primacy attributed to the passions? It perhaps connects to the view that we are descended from animals, and that animal nature is basically one of passions and appetites, the beasts have no (or very little) reason. The emancipation of man from the dark forces of his animal nature, from his base passions and lusts, the realization of his capacity to free and

27

enlighten himself, to create art, culture and civilization all had to do with his cultivation of his potential for reason.

1.4 Anthropology and rationality

So the earliest academic anthropology, especially in the hands of Tylor and Frazer, was closely allied with the rationalist tradition, and this continued to be the case with the *Année Sociologique* writers around Durkheim, and their English followers Radcliffe-Brown and Malinowski. To all these thinkers one of the basic questions was the extent of the rationality of man, and particularly of primitive man. Anthropologists were not simply engaged in cataloguing the welter of man's superstitious follies. Rather their work refuted older views that savages were just wild-eyed and irrational, possibly not even capable of language, still less reasoning. Languages, cultures, social arrangements, and so on, perhaps not easy to fathom, were nevertheless to be found among remote and savage peoples. The primitive and the modern were linked, not sharply differentiated. The simplest hypothesis to accommodate this vision was to try to order societies as attempts of varying success to realize their rational potential, hence to be some steps on the way to 'real' civilization and culture. If this was the model of the structure of man's nature, then anthropology ventured to apply this structure to history. Beasts were earlier than men. Then the question is, how did the transition from the one to the other take place? How did savage early man become civilized modern man? How did reason win over passion?

One particular version of this general view, evolutionism, theorizes that rationality, the capacity to overcome the obstacles of emotion and superstition and to learn better from experience, emerges over time. Thus evolutionism allows that primitive societies can be arranged along a time scale depending upon at which 'stage' of the emergence of rationality they appear to be. Another version, but logically the same view, is that the scale should be spatial rather than temporal: that manifestations of accelerated rational learning such as technology, culture and the like diffuse outward from centres of innovation and hence that societies can be located on radii originating at such centres or sources. On one scale social forms emerged gradually over time; on the other, social forms diffused slowly over space. Whether temporal or spatial evolution was adopted, the main task of anthropology became that of arranging recorded and still extant human societies along a scale. Arguments about what scales to employ and about where individual societies should be placed on those scales constituted much of the theoretical literature of anthropology.

Unfortunately, both evolutionism and diffusionism faced a problem with units. Neither cultures nor societies were very manageable units in terms of which to think; what seemed to evolve or diffuse were fragments like customs, traits or institutions. But if that line of argument is pursued a society comes to be thought of as incoherent. Instead of being an integral whole we envisage it as a disparate collection of all sorts of traits, some evolved, some retarded, some diffused, others not diffused, and so on. Yet anthropological experience was that societies did not readily lend themselves to conceptual decomposition in this way. On the contrary, they struck observers as functioning fairly well as integrated wholes. Hence the entire notion of mankind evolving or diffusing improved realization of its rational capacities became suspect.

It also became suspect for another and rather different reason. The evolutionist and diffusionist systems of ordering societies had praise/blame implicit in them: the assumption that it is better to possess a diffused innovation than to have missed it; it is better to be evolved than not to be. But it seemed more than coincidence that these scales just somehow or other took as their benchmarks for praise/blame the advanced industrial societies of Europe and North America. Anthropology was self-serving: it elevated the societies it sprang from to the heights. Modern industrial society is the measure of all things. This posture could be sustained only so long as anthropology based itself largely on the reports of travellers, traders, missionaries and colonial officials, all of whom had a vested interest in wearing certain sorts of blinkers. But with the innovation of the field expedition, one that diffused or evolved in anthropology over a long period of time, new kinds of evidence and new ways of looking at evidence emerged.

Anthropologists proved in fieldwork practice that it was possible for a modern western man to live his life among strange people; to find order and coherence there; also language and oral as well as material culture; and, ultimately, things to admire and praise. This was not to be confused with romanticizing the savage – an old, old, outlook. This was rather giving the savage his due for: his capacity to survive in seemingly harsh or threatening environments; for his maintenance of balance with nature; for his special solutions to the problems of human life (alternative kinship systems, for example) and death; for his philosophy. Once humanized in this way, once taken out of the role of specimen, or earlier stage, the reality of other cultures and societies threatened the entire system of thinking behind anthropology. No longer could the anthropologist's own society be taken as a benchmark in the evolution or the diffusion of culture, civilization, rationality. On the contrary, other societies could be used as benchmarks, or the very notion of benchmarks against which others were to be weighed in the balance and found wanting could be put under siege.

1.5 The centrality of belief and science

Culture or society of course consisted in many sorts of things. It is a significant fact that the debate has focussed always around not culture or society in general but around systems of belief, those we usually call science and religion. Why so? Because science and religion focus the issue of rationality—applying reason to the task of learning about reason—very sharply. Last-ditch defenders of western industrial civilization (the culture of science and of anthropology) as a benchmark, and here I would include myself, along with Gellner (1964, 1975), Agassi (1975, 1977, 1981), and others, look to the rise of the (western) science of nature and of man, including anthropology itself, as a dramatic breakthrough in the history of mankind's rationality. We pick out the capacity to learn from experience as the key indicator of the rationality of man, and science as the supreme achievement in learning from experience. Notice how this sociologizes the issue of rationality. Individual men are not ranked by rational capacity, social formations are. Science is an institution that functions to facilitate learning from experience. Societies also have other institutions for learning from experience, folk wisdom, religion, magic, and so on. These function less effectively than science in many respects so the presence of science and the degree of its diffusion and cultivation within a society are some sort of measure, however crude in practice, of achieved rationality.

Science certainly didn't come to us as a bolt from the muse. It was gained by a combination of hard reflection and lucky inspiration. Its consequences for us include an immensely increased power over our ecological niche, over ourselves, and a paradigm case of what man's rational potential is like. All this may go some way to explain why the debate about rationality has in recent years so vigorously centred around the beliefs we class as magic, science, and religion, and especially around the rationality of these systems of thought, belief and social organization.[7]

The rationalists among us tend towards the view that it is the qualities of universality, transcendence, and social neutrality that are the merits and ideals of a system that is genuinely learning from experience.

Science is the emblem: it gives us knowledge of sticks and stones, tides and moons, kinship systems and psyches regardless of from which society these things are seen, regardless of traditional doctrines on these matters, regardless of in which vested interests and in which groups there may be opposing views. It is egalitarian in Bacon's sense, because it operates a model of learning from experience in which every person can participate: rationality is externalized in the social organization not internalized in individual capacity.

Earlier attempts to characterize the rationality of science focussed not on Bacon's social ideas but on the philosophy of empiricism, the doctrine that science is rational because it argues from a direct appeal to sense experience, experience that all rational men have. This was a bold and brilliant philosophy that, however, even Bacon discovered had serious deficiencies. With the relocation of rationality in social organization rather than psychology, some rehabilitation was possible. Popper proposed a sophisticated version of empiricism that said we don't argue *from* simple universal sense experience, but that we do argue *with* the help of simple universal sense experience (1959). The rules of argument that we use constitute a very elementary and intuitive logic, based on the ideas of negation and contradiction. Like sense experience, elementary logic is easy to resist, but not easy to ignore. We build institutional embodiments of these and other rules, and also procedures for improving the rules and these constitute the social institution of science: rationality socially realized. Gellner has taken another step and tried to show the extent to which the kind of society science fits into constitutes a decisive break with traditional social forms.

Here was an important new move: traditional thought goes with traditional social forms. Traditional social forms have a tendency to stasis: to make the accommodation to the ecological niche and stay in balance with it. Thus beliefs about the natural and the supernatural world will be one continuous field that is, moreover, tied down to features of the local environment. A cave here, a mountain there, certain persons, particular rites, local knowledge, hierarchy, taboos and so on are connected to accounts of why things happen. Such a system of thought has a kind of rationality, but it is a weak kind. It is weak in relation to stronger kinds that transcend, incorporate and correct this local one.

Evans-Pritchard showed in *Witchcraft, Oracles and Magic Among the Azande* that Azande have quite reasonable-sounding arguments to dispose of the failures of their magic or of scepticism directed towards it. Inspired by this great classic, Agassi and I (1967) suggested viewing the rationality of the Azande as *weak*. A *stronger* form would propose that a system of belief was rational if it incorporated some standard for the evaluation of beliefs. The strongest form of rationality would be that which incorporated the highest standards. Stronger forms could themselves be subdivided. Any acknowledged standard is stronger than an unacknowledged, implicit or absent one. But there remains the possibility of a very strong or strongest standard which embodies the most critically assessed.

Gellner's view is not dissimilar. He envisages four ways in which modern scientific thought demands higher standards of rational appraisal than is traditional: by cognitive division of labour, by absence of entrenched clauses, by ideas not being judges in their own cause and by mechanism (Gellner 1973b, 1975: see also § 3.2 below).

Science seen in this way is the embodiment of rationality, a cognitive and also an institutional embodiment. The latter in a way controls the former. The task of learning from experience, the task of being the living species that may in some limited way gain control of its own destiny in the way that gases, stars, plants and other animals could not, is a co-operative task depending upon the creation of social forms that foster the process of learning from learning from experience.

1.6 Anti-cognitive views of magic and religion

Arrayed against even such a mildly scientific picture of rationality nowadays is a motley collection of philosophies of anthropology, all more or less apologetic for traditional societies and confused about science and rationality. Common to many of them is a resistance to seeing science as a benchmark of human achievement. Some suggest that the emotional, aesthetic and religious achievements of man are as important, as worthy, as his scientific endeavours, and should therefore equally be used as benchmarks. But if the issue is rationality not much is gained by raising the question of what is so great about rationality anyway. We can leave that question for another place. It will be fairly obvious what partisans of rationality as I have outlined it are going to say to this line of thought. Without decrying the emotions, it can be said that they are only sometimes a good guide to action, action aimed at survival, prosperity, aesthetic or religious achievement. They are very limited and very primitive guides to life, and our rationality is perhaps measured by our learning to cope with our emotions, that is, assess them as guides to action. Anger, for example, may need to be expressed rather than repressed, but the manner of its expression needs to be thought about. However satisfying its expression at the time, if it leads to destruction of our own or other's precious property, or to the alienation of those we care about, or to severe social sanctions, then we can learn that its expression had better be carefully channelled. Sometimes we allow inchoate feelings about people to control our actions when trusting them, accepting their information, or loving them. This too can be a mistake, since inchoate feelings may embody naïveté or the possibility of being duped, or a failure to anticipate ways in which the person will change and hence behave in the future.

All these self-corrections have to be learned in a spirit of self-preservation. This suggests one can have a rationalist (or cognitive) theory of the emotions that assumes we have very little inherent or instinctive emotional equipment, and that what we have needs refinement and correction in the light of experience. This is why mankind rises not just above the beasts, but also above itself, i.e. its own past sanguinary history.

The emotional history and anthropology of mankind is not to be ignored, for it too has a rational side and evinces signs of progress. Many emotions that individual men stand by and that societies endorse are despicable. Our ability to see this and to explain why shows that we are capable of moral progress. Moral progress is no more inevitable, irreversible, monolithic or unilinear than evolutionary or scientific progress. But it is a rational fact of anthropology.

Aesthetic achievement is a rather different matter. We seem unsure as to whether there is progress in art (Gombrich 1961). That is, whether changes in art result in a new that is somehow better than the old. Icons are not less appreciated after the invention of perspective, representational art is not less appreciated after the advent of abstraction. Moreover, while not denying the aesthetic aspect of social forms (anthropologists often remark on the symmetry and elegance of segmentary lineage systems), there are other measures of them, such as their stability, flexibility, effectiveness in facilitating the realization of social and individual goals, their capacity to promote learning and hence self-correction from experience.

Now comes the turn of those specific social forms of magic and religion. We can consider their moral and aesthetic as well as rational aspects. It was the genius of Tylor and Frazer to realize that in the quest to understand man's rationality and the history of its growth, it was systems of thought, putative cognitions, on which the issues should turn. It was their vision to collect together myths, stories, legends, magical ideas, religious cosmologies and natural science into one conceptual box, there to be sorted out and arranged. They made this bold leap of thought despite the fact that Greek myths and nuclear physics are hardly embodied in the same sorts of social context and hence hardly perform the same social functions and very certainly do not have attached anything like similar sorts of rituals and social enactments. Their emotional resonance, aesthetic value and social embedding may or may not be similar, but this is no barrier to assessing their rationality.

Before I can discuss magic and religion as putative cognition, however, I must note the objections of those who flatly deny the Tylor-Frazer premiss that magic or religion are in any significant way cognitive efforts. There are elements of revisionism and apologetics in this denial, for it seems to me quite obvious that in the past religions have put forward claims to cognition, as when the Bible was taken to contain all true knowledge, even down to its creation stories, geographical muddles, and chronological absurdities. It and the Koran are still to this day taken as sources of knowledge by partisans who may be somewhat less sophisticated than anthropologists.

I shall not stress this ahistorical and apologetic character of the denial, however. Rather am I interested in once again challenging those anthropologists who try to make a case for some qualitative difference between systems of superstitious thought and science. One of their lines of approach is that religion and magic operate at the affectual rather than the rational level in the human mind. Another is that religion and magic have little or no technological intent, since if they manipulate at all it is either abstractions or spirits, or a handful of medicines, charms and the like. A third is that, however similar they look, religion and magic are different from cognition in a very clear way: they operate to symbolize and express things, rather than to analyse, dissect, explain and control them, their written expressions resemble poems more than scientific papers.

On the affectual side of religion I would not deny it but add that science operates on the affectual level too. The question is whether there is also a cognitive side to religion. No one denies either that man has emotions, or that these emotions are very important. One of his strongest emotions is that of wanting to understand and control. When he says a prayer or performs a spell he emotionally addresses the world, as well as his gods and other forces. His emotion of love of god and nature may be no less expressed when he sends alpha particles hurtling towards a nucleus.

To the extent that any sharp birfucation of man's soul into affectual, appetitive and intellectual is presupposed by the idea that religion is emotional, then it seems naive. Men are whole, not divided, and I have already tried to argue the point that the rationality of learning from experience is not detached from the emotions. The emotional level, so-called, may be a component of the intellectual level. Our mental equipment when we set out on life's journey consists of the capacity to organize our perceptual experience, to experience strong feelings in relation to ourselves and our states, and of a further capacity to modify both our cognitive and emotional states as the world impacts upon us. Even if primarily affectual, religion cannot be without cognitive content.

When Christians and savages pray for rain, or for the hostages in Iran, one interpretation says simply that they hope some mechanism called God will effect their desires. More sophisticated religious thinkers are embarrassed by this wizard-with-the-white-beard-in-the-sky notion, and try to find ways of interpreting such acts as simply outpourings of yearning and love, acknowledgment of subordination to the deity, etc.[8] Side-stepping the possibility of disingenuous apologetics (always present) the argument here is clear enough. If someone is overhead imploring someone else to do something for him, then we are allowed to conclude that he believes that effectively this outcome is possible for this someone. To ask someone to do something implies at the very least that it can be done, and furthermore that it can be done by the requested.

It is sometimes argued at this point that the inference to efficacy cannot be made because the words being uttered or the ceremony performed may be one the performer does as a matter of tradition or of routine, totally unaware of its cognitive content in the required sense (as when it is performed in an archaic or strange language). This argument is irrelevant. Conscious intention is not required for the inference. When I say to rain dancers that experience shows that rain dancing is not a very effective way to bring rain, but that cloud-seeding has a better chance of success, I am advocating learning from experience about rain-making. If they then reply that they aren't trying to bring rain but are practising for next week's rodeo at which their aim is to earn money, I shall say fine. If they say instead that's all very well but that this is a central ceremony in their tribe's culture, and to perform it and keep it alive and teach it to their children is part of affirming their identity, culture, etc., I shall say fine. But if at the backs of their minds they have a sneaking suspicion there is a rain spirit, or if their culture once held that to be so, then I shall press. But again, if they say, let's seed clouds *and* rain dance for insurance, who will object? So long as they have the surplus resources to afford both there is no argument against them doing whatever they want.

Behind this argument about the relative unimportance of any technological intent to magic and religion lies a series of suppressed premisses that bedevils the dispute and which should be brought out. The main premiss is the reduction of science to technology, or the identifying of technology with a very important part of science. It seems to me that it is important to separate the aspiration of science, which is universal and transcendental cognition, from its great side-benefit, which is technological power over the world.[9] The parallel between magic, religion and science would stand even if science had no technological component. The parallel is that they are all attempts at cognition – i.e. at knowing how the world is – whatever else they do or are. Pure science is the attempt to put forward conjectures that make sense of experience, and then to check those conjectures against experience. Many of those conjectures may not yield technological consequences at all, as in the case of plate tectonics, or theories of the formation and physical processes of the stars, or the general theory of evolution. The predictions we derive from such theories are checked against other experience, not used to build machines. Technology is often said to be based on out-of-date science, since the working and limitations of out-of-date science are better understood than that of current science. Hence the absence of any technological component or intent in religion and magic would be irrelevant.

This said, we can come closer to the heart of the matter. For the apologist may concede a cognitive component to magic and religion but play it down as unimportant. What is important is said to be the expressive and symbolic intent of magic and religion, and this cannot be described and judged by the criteria applied to putative cognition, such as testability, but rather by such as functionality or the aesthetic. At first this argument was put forward *sotto voce*, as a way of escaping the harsh conclusion of the magic, religion, science evolution, and perhaps also to explain why magic and religion persist. If there is continuity between magic, religion and science, then cognitive and technological criteria can be applied to the evaluation of all three. By these criteria magic and religion are going to be found sorely wanting compared to science. Indeed, the implication is going to be obvious that our rationality dictates that when we have science we do not need the ur-sciences magic and religion. Then the persistence can be explained by their symbolic and aesthetic appeal but they do not have to be taken seriously by the rationalist.

Perhaps such an explanation of the persistence of magic and religion is unnecessary. The rise of new technology does not always displace older forms, they often coexist (bicycles and cars; gramophones and tape recorders; houses and apartments); the same is true of social forms (monarchies and republics; various

taxes); of mathematics; of scientific calculation; etc. The persistence of magic and religion is not in need of explanation merely
because of the rise of science. But their persistence is not a sign
of rational merit. Durkheim's argument that religion cannot be
sheer error because otherwise it would not be universal[10] is
premissed on the absurdly optimistic doctrine that there is a self-
correcting process that will not allow everyone to believe an error.
There is the possibility of correction, but it is not automatic.
Facts underdetermine theories, as inductivists say. Better put,
the known facts are always compatible with a range of theories.
Probably the whole world once thought the earth was flat, yet
that is not only an error, somewhere along the way those believers
found a way to break out of the self-reinforcing circle and discover
the error.

The latest moves regarding the symbolic and aesthetic defences
of magic and religion seem to go even further than Durkheim –
we should take symbolism and the aesthetic seriously because
they are universal. We are told all human society and interaction
consists of systems of expression and symbolism, that science itself
is, as it were, simply a further poetic ordering or symbolizing to
which some of us accord special status because it pleases our
aesthetic taste. This argument points us towards the topic of relativism which will occupy the second part of this monograph. At
this stage it is to be looked at from the point of view of rationality.
To compare magic and religion either to the expression of
emotions, or to a work of art, is all very well provided we also
stress the extent to which science too is expressive and aesthetic.
Scientific conjectures come we know not whence. Einstein
accepted Popper's comparison of his vision of the universe to that
of the ancient poet Parmenides, indeed he accepted that they
were identical, although one was expressed in Ancient Greek, the
other in scientific German and advanced mathematics (Popper
1974, p. 102). Einstein also spoke of science as an intellectual
union with experience, and Russell, as we have seen, expressed
the yearning for union with the harmonies of the universe. These
are explanations of the beauty and the emotional satisfaction of
doing science, just as they are of doing magic or religion. The
harmony and ordering of events carries an emotional kick, possibly because of fear of chaos.

Having reversed the argument, and conceded the symbolic and
aesthetic side of science, perhaps now the cognitive and technological claims of magic and religion can be faced too. They are
both explicit and implicit. To play them down is to distort magic
and religion as much as to play down the symbolic and aesthetic
is to distort science.

But is that the end of it? Well, for one thing, all that I have so far said is quite rational. For another, there is a lack of methodological naïveté in the symbolist account of magic and religion. What is methodological naïveté? The principle of methodological naïveté says *don't listen to what people say, look at what they do.* It is well established in anthropology. Well, here they are doing a rain dance. Not symbolizing. Dancing. I offer a different methodological principle that says, what people say they are doing should be taken at its face value unless there are good reasons for not doing so. Applying this, we must allow cognitive and technological aims to magic and religion.

What is going on here, why is there resistance to treating magic and religion as cognitive systems? Why does so much of the argument about human rationality turn on the relation of science to primitive thought? Well, unlike science, which despite its diverse history, has a tendency to converge on current knowledge, systems of magic and religion proliferate chaotically the world over. Furthermore, these systems offer strong and direct challenges to the simple model of rationality as learning from experience that I have offered. Magical and religious systems are known, for instance, to deny elementary logical principles, such as that of contradiction; they are known to claim that the only genuine knowledge of reality is gained through religious or mystical enlightenment and is a state of being rather than a state of mind; in short, as cognitive systems, magic and religion are rather poor. But then, are we not denigrating those who hold such beliefs? Not just savages, but the Christians and Jews among anthropologists themselves? The motive, then, for resisting the cognitive continuity of magic, religion and science is that it embarrasses those anthropologists who are not themselves free of superstition and religion.

Their embarrassment is easy to understand. Few of us can claim to be free of ancestral superstition and awe of ancient myths. I have been a conscious atheist since my mid-teens, yet I recall observing with some amusement that the more blatantly blasphemous scenes in *Monty Python's Life of Brian* made the hairs on my neck prickle. What may be a difference between rationalists and apologists is the very attitude of wishing to learn from experience, hence to be self-critical, to face and overcome ancestral superstition. One need not deny the potency and staying power of these things, the question is whether one wants to be in thrall to that.

Those in thrall to them are not inferior or lesser beings, still less primitives or savages. What they are is less rational than it is possible to be. If they are unaware of the possibilities, as many anthropological subjects are, we may think of them as at a stage they sooner or later will go beyond. If they are aware of the stronger rationality that is possible then they are being inconsistent.

1. Digression: rationality and racialism

The doctrine that man is the rational animal has a counterpart or parts that might be formulated like this:

All men are rational but some are more rational than others

or,

judging by their lesser rationality, not all seeming-men are men.

What I have formulated here are two versions of racialism: the idea that mankind is divided into naturally distinct races (Stepan 1982, p. xx) and that these races can be arranged on a scale of rationality. Extreme racialists drop some races off the end of the scale of human beings altogether, classing them as orang-outangs (Nott and Gliddon 1854, Winchell 1880), or what not, but this is not logically necessary within racialism. Only the grading is necessary. Not even the correlations with skin colour, cephalic index, temperament or other features is necessary.

According both to the historian Lewis Hanke and the philosopher and historian of ideas Richard Popkin, modern ideas of race are indeed modern. Without denying Popper's speculative claim (1945, ch. 8, sects. I, II) that Plato's theory of the metallic bases of our souls is a direct progenitor of racialist ideas, they contend that Christianity had an alternative monogenetic account of mankind, descended from Adam and then again from Noah. Each of these scholars has pursued independent lines of thought into the re-birth of racialism in modern times. For Hanke one could say the decisive event was the discovery of the New World. For there, far away from all known civilization and the probable descendants of Noah, there lived man-like creatures. If they were men then they had reason and could receive the truth of Christianity. If they were man-like beasts without reason then they could be treated as slaves or even animals.

The decisive event for Popkin is not the New World as such but the researches of an obscure seventeenth-century thinker called Isaac de la Péyrère who may have been the first important discoverer of inconsistencies in Genesis, and who drew the conclusion that there was more than one creation. After slaying Abel, Cain went away to the East of Eden and married and produced a tribe. So there had to have been men before Adam. Where were these creatures? Perhaps they had been found in North America.

Hanke's contribution is summarized in three books (1949, 1959 and 1974) all decorated with the same frontispiece picture of his hero Don Bartholomé de las Casas, Dominican, Bishop of Chiapa and Apostle to the Indians. Las Casas's nemesis was Juan Gines de Sepulveda, a scholar. They were to confront each other in 1550 in a formal debate before the King of Spain's Council on the Indies to debate the moral basis of the Spanish Conquest. By force of arms, Spain was colonizing the Indies, indenturing the Indians to work in the mines, and enslaving some. The question was whether these were potentially Christian men and women of rational capacity. Simplifying in a way that doubtless would make Hanke cringe, one could say that Las Casas's view was that all mankind is one and the Indians deserved respect, consideration and conversion to bring them along to civilization; while Sepulveda regarded them as lacking culture and law, being eaters of human flesh, inferior to Spaniards, skilled only at a level that bears comparison with birds and spiders. They are not devoid of reason and so their irreligion is wicked and they should be justly subjugated by a pious and just king.

> Of all the ideas churned up during the early tumultuous years of American history, none had a more dramatic application than the attempts made to apply to the natives there the Aristotelian doctrine of natural slavery: that one part of mankind is set aside by nature to be slaves in the service of masters born for a life of virtue free of manual labour.
> (Hanke 1959, pp. 12–13)

There was some urgency to the question, since the Spanish conquest of the Indies was proceeding apace and rules for its conduct were required and there was the possibility that the discovery and conquest of the New World forecast the end of the world and the coming of the millennial kingdom. The question was, then, could the Indians be converted and, if they could, should reason be mingled with force? Francisco de Vitoria wrote:

> The Indian aborigines . . . are not of unsound mind, but have, according to their kind, the use of reason. This is clear, because there is a certain method in their affairs; they have polities which are carefully arranged and they have definite marriage and magistrates, overlords, laws, and workshops, and a system of exchange, all of which call for the use of

reason; they also have a kind of religion. (Hanke 1959, pp. 22-3)

Protracted debate between Sepulveda and Las Casas at Valladolid in 1550 failed to produce a clear judgment, some of the judges dying without submitting their opinions. But this fact has an apt irony. Even today the problem of the relations between unlike cultures and races is a vexed one. The pieties and the rhetoric tend to be the same, the practice and the intellectual confusion also. Aristotle's own ideas are unclear and contradictory. His most famous pupil, Alexander the Great, is credited by some historians as being the first person known to us to contemplate the brotherhood of man or the unity of mankind.

From Valladolid to the United Nations Declaration of Human Rights there stretches, according to Hanke, one road. Those spirits, such as Alexander and Las Casas, who argued for equal dignity for all men were opposed, not only by Aristotelians and racialists within western Christendom, but by the insularity and prejudices of the encountered natives too. One of the most sickening pieties of the guilt-ridden free world is the idea that people in what we now call the Third World are enlightened and tolerant people of nature. Anthropologists tend not to stress it, but they do report clearly that, speaking generally, native peoples evince curiosity and envy of other cultures, but rarely high valuation. In fact often enough they display naked prejudice and contempt towards those of other cultures. This, one might say, does not make it easier to adopt tolerance in practice.

After Valladolid, and indeed until today, the problem of the basic nature of other peoples different from ourselves in colour, race, religion, or customs has given rise to the most diverse and often inflammatory opinions. It might be said that the idea of the unfitness of natives and their inferiority to Europeans appeared in whatever far corners of the world Europeans reached. Protestants as well as Catholics found themselves embroiled in these questions and afflicted with the same doubts. The French missionaries sent by Calvin to Brazil a few years after Sepulveda's 1550 attack on Indians found the natives difficult to work with and came to doubt whether they could ever become true members of their faith.

Englishmen, too, adopted what might be called the standard cliché on Indian nature; William Cunningham, in one of the earliest descriptions of Indians to appear in England, had this to say in 1559: 'The people bothe men and women are naked, neither suffer they any heare to growe on their bodies, no not on their browes, the head excepte . . . They is no law or

41

order observed of wedlocke, for it is lawful to have so many women as they affect, and to put them away with out any daunger. They be filthy at meate, and in all secrete acts of nature, comparable to brute beastes.' (Hanke 1959, p. 99)

Hence the same questions were faced by European colonists in Africa, India, Australia and so on, and time and again outrages were justified by appeal to the natives' lack of or inadequate rationality, their resemblance to beasts. Beasts of burden have a value, and should obviously be cared for within limits, but, it was argued, it would be as difficult for an Australian aboriginal to accept civilization as for a monkey to understand a problem of Euclid. This was written in the mid-nineteenth century by an early anthropologist. Yet in 1550 a Spanish friar was arguing:

Thus mankind is one, and all men are alike in that which concerns their creation, and no one is born enlightened. From this it follows that all of us must be guided and aided at first by those who were born before us. And the savage people of the earth may be compared to uncultivated soil that readily brings forth weeds and useless thorns, but has within itself such natural virtue that by labour and cultivation it may be made to yield sound and beneficial fruits. (Hanke 1959, p. 112)

It would be glib to dismiss this as condescending. In an ethnocentric world it is about as enlightened as almost anyone ever gets: we nearly all think our way of life is best, else why would we cleave to it in the face of evidence of alternatives? So in a *chacun a son goût* spirit we preach tolerance. But rationality is not just a matter of *goût*, it is connected to such things as knowledge. The things some cultures do are premissed on putative knowledge of others. We thus see how the problems of culture contact are also the problems of culture clash, and that these have deep historical roots, and current practical application.

In the course of trying, for more than a decade, to show the centrality in the emergence of the modern secular world view of Isaac de la Péyrère, Richard Popkin (1974b) has shown how the philosophical roots of modern racialism trace to the same source. Popkin contends that modern racialism began with the practice of issuing certificates of 'purity of blood' to fifteenth-century Spanish Christians to attest that they were free of the contamination of former and forcibly converted Jews. Although converted, Jews were thought to have ineradicable biological and spiritual characteristics that could lead to subversive or destructive behaviour.

Coincidentally, it was the Spanish who conquered the New

World and had to make their minds up about the Indians. Evidence against their full humanity was their alleged incapacity to have abstract ideas, not running their own affairs properly and immoral behaviour. One biological mark was skin colour, a mark of God's curse and hence of inherent inferiority. Like 'Jewish Blood', it could not be assimilated away. The trouble was that the Biblical account of human creation is monogenist – singular. All humans are from one stock, Adam, or, more strictly, Noah. An inherent division in the nature of mankind needs careful explanation. A polygenist account, while not Biblical, is easier to work out.

Much ink, from Locke on, was spilled on degeneracy theories while Linnaeus, Buffon and others leaned towards climate as the explanation of the degeneration. Degenerationists split over whether it was irreversible or could, with enlightened treatment and conversion, be overcome. Popkin calls the latter 'liberal racism' (p. 138); I would call it condescension which still affirms the rational unity of mankind. This the polygenists denied. Although they thought of themselves as scientists, they yet believed the Bible was the history of Jews and whites – all peoples of colour were pre-Adamites, irremediably different and inferior (see also Stanton 1960). Shocked by all this, as well as by the racialism of Hume, Voltaire, Goethe and so on, Popkin proclaims that only a thorough going cultural relativism will overcome our racialist heritage (1974b, pp. 151–72). He quite underplays a central weakness of polygenism, namely the problem of inter-breeding. Although humankind has diverse origins, all its members can interbreed and hence by Buffon's test we are one species. If, however, the species has weak and strong, degenerate and vigorous strains, why not breed up? Here racialists offer *ad hoc* suggestions about the special degeneracy of half-breeds and mulattoes combining the worst of both strains (Hunt 1863) and hence, more to the point, interbreeding and intermarriage can be outlawed. Western society has split on this – the Catholic colonialists on the whole approving intermarriage, the Protestants not. But the Dutch, encouraging it while their descendants in South Africa banned it, show that no simple dichotomy works.

The other weakness of Popkin's account is that it makes no mention of racialism other than European. He writes as though it was a terrible doctrine the colonizers visited on the colonized. But as his allusions to Jews should indicate, racialist western colonizers met their match in the ideas of some of their subject peoples. Inter-racial sex and marriage looked no prettier to Hindu Brahmans or Chinese Mandarins than it did to white men. It is a European illusion that black people in Africa covet white flesh.

43

1.8 Cargo cults as an illustration

Let me now backtrack somewhat and come over these points on beliefs and science again with the help of an example: cargo cults.

'Cargo cults' is the name given to cult movements observed among the native peoples of the widely scattered islands of the South-West Pacific known as Melanesia. Characteristically some people would be stirred up by a prophet, a person of no previous status or importance[11] whose prophecy offered a highly untraditional vision of the future. The message usually concerned the welfare and fate of the native peoples. These were predicted to improve, and two longed-for events would occur: shipments of the sorts of consumer goods that usually went only to Europeans would arrive for the Melanesians, and the tribal ancestors would return. Material consumer goods are called *kago* in pidgin, obviously from ships' *cargo*. These cults had many local variations, sometimes involving only a few faithful, other times huge numbers actively taking part over many years. They occurred on islands widely separated from one another by vast stretches of empty ocean. They often predicted specific points in time when the cargo could arrive, and yet they would continue only slightly modified when those predictions did not turn out to be true.

The recurrence of the cults and the sometimes bizarre behaviour of the cultists (e.g. frenzied dancing or talking in unintelligible language) led some white men to dismiss them as 'irrational', indeed as mad. The first book on the cults was by F. E. Williams, a colonial official in Papua. Titled *The Vailala Madness*, it appeared in 1923. Williams's view was that cargo cults were a mysterious kind of fit which came upon the natives because of 'mental confusion'. This fit spread unless the natives were handled with 'firmness' (the English prefect coming out in the District Commissioner). At the time Williams wrote there was some thought that the Vailala madness was an isolated occurrence. When, however, the Second World War came to Melanesia, in the form of troops and equipment of all nations, the cargo cult crystallized in anthropologists' minds into a special form of millennarian religion. Special cargo, arrival preparations, spirits of the dead, inversion of present social forms, gave them a unique flavour. American anthropologists classed them, and explained them, as 'acculturation movements'. They saw the cults as attempts to come to terms with the West, the product of culture shock and hence of a sort of irrational confusion of behaviour, similar to the 'nativism' of the Ghost Dance, amongst the Plains Indians,[12] but moving towards rather than away from the intruder. The problem producing the cults was thought to be native envy of the more powerful culture coupled with inability to understand how it worked. The natives feel 'deprived' and so attempt to rectify this by inadequate and even irrational means.

Working purely from library materials, Peter Worsley (1957) proposed the theory that the cargo cults were incipient political movements, arising, in classic Marxist way, amongst an oppressed and exploited working class scattered the length and breadth of Melanesia, their class consciousness having been raised by the advent of Japanese invaders (coloured but powerful), American counter-attackers (plentiful material goods and racially mixed), the displacement of the old colonial authorities (British, French, German), etc. Finally the exploited rebel, the oppressed protest. As in the Middle Ages, this often took the form of millenarian religion. Later, a transition to political forms and nationalism can be expected.[13]

Another classical commentary on the cults was by Kenelm Burridge who saw them more as emphasizing aspirations to spiritual and moral equality, the desire to be real men as Europeans are. This is expressed in various ways in the myth-dream of the cult. To each of these theories counter-examples could be given – other areas with oppression, with deprivation, with spiritual and moral inequality which did not have cargo cults. Unexplained, the cargo cults seemed little more rational than the Vailala Madness. Light really began to appear only when Hogbin (1958), Belshaw (1950, 1954) and Lawrence (1964) pulled the evidence together and suggested that cargo cults were entirely rational once the logic of Melanesian society and its traditions was grasped. Set the native in his culture, environment and systems of belief, including a tradition of messianic religions, colonial authorities, the magical perfection of manufactured goods, the disruptions brought on by wage labour, the profferring of Christianity, trade, and you can come up with a series of conjectures as to how to manipulate the world and the Europeans to get what is desired. What is desired is a mix of the old, e.g. the return of the spirits of the dead (sorely missed), and the new, e.g. European goods and moral, social and spiritual equality with the colonialists.

In a long study of the literature on Melanesian cargo cults published twenty years ago (Jarvie 1964a), I found that many attempts had been made to explain them, which meant many attempts had been made either to give an account of them that preserved the rationality of the actors, or to give an account of them that abandoned the rationality of the actors. As to the latter: to attribute systematic, patterned and widespread cargo-cult behaviour to madness or irrationality was, I argued, no explanation at all. To declare action goal-less or not displaying rationality

45

is not specific but compatible with virtually any behaviour. So, the question remained of why *this* kind of action, namely messianic religious cults of relatively short duration, and relatively constant patterns, rather than any other actions.

Two rationality-preserving explanations were functionalism and Marxism. Functionalist explanations were wanting, I argued, because of the novelty and open-endedness of the cults; they could not be 'fitted' into a neat feed-back loop of reinforcing social integration. Marxist explanations were provocative, since they attempted to construct the logic of the situation, namely that of colonial oppression and exploitation, which would render cult activity a case of applying reason to the task of understanding and resistance. But they concentrated on the political and military overtones and had difficulty explaining the religious character of the cults. At best Marxists reduced the cults to precursors of political liberation movements. Much of Melanesia has been peacefully de-colonized and cargo cultists have not emerged into the national political process, although cults and elections have become mixed up.

My own explanatory conjecture about cargo cults was that they were attempts to learn about the world from experience, the better to thrive in it. Hence they were at least weakly rational. I picture the situation of the cult-prone peoples on isolated islands or in remote valleys coming into contact with the white man and his wealth. Coveting some of the things the white man had, especially those that seemed to give him power over nature, attempts were made to apply reason to the task of procuring this sort of material for Melanesians. The obstacle to success was that the white man came ready-equipped with his cargo goods, and the processes of procurement and what we call manufacture were unclear. Conjecturing on the basis of their own society's stock of knowledge, Melanesians concluded that most of the goods were made by spirits (whence their perfection), and that the white man either had a superior standing with the spirits and hence great attention should be paid to his ceremonies in order to gain that same standing, or else the white man had intercepted and misappropriated goods intended for the Melanesians, and the spirits needed to be reminded of this and asked to intercede to restore the goods to those they were intended for.[14]

I more or less left it at that. To conjecture that this process of applying reason to the task of understanding their impoverished situation would gradually ease the Melanesians towards a correct understanding of white wealth and how consumer durables were to be acquired would have been optimistic. Religious cycles of rise and fall, renewal, rise and fall again, could easily go on indefinitely, because the stock of beliefs that were in the background of all cult thinking could function very like Collingwood's 'absolute presuppositions' of an age, and be both constrainingly inescapable and invisible.[15] Experience as such is not sufficient to undermine an entire quasi-religious cosmology.[16] However, it did seem to me that repeated failures of the cults and persistent contact with white men who were, after all, offering their own alternate explanation of their wealth and their manufacturing processes, could in the end just possibly percolate down.

To my delight, not long after I had published all this in a methodological study of anthropology, an Australian anthropologist, Peter Lawrence, with whose work I was already familiar from papers, published a detailed study of successive waves of cult activity in one area (Lawrence 1964). His interpretation was that, despite some slippage, there was developing over time in that area a better and better approximation to what we should call the truth of the matter. Successive prophets and their cults were approaching more closely to a correct understanding of the situation. The only thing to add would be that as the cultists' efforts asymptotically approach the truth – which is that the trade goods are manufactured by men and not by spirits, by mechanical processes that are not mysterious, however different they are from those who work only with wood and stone, and that wealth comes from division of labour and accumulation of capital – then the less religious those ideas would become and the less ritualized the actions would become, the more commonsensical-sounding native ideas and hence actions would become.

So what can be expected to happen on my account of cargo cults is that a phenomenon so bizarre as to be widely held up as such, is first reduced to a weak rationality. It is allowed that the actions have goals. That is to say, a religious response to material wants is declared understandable in a culture where cognition is univocal, folding together elements we would distinguish as religious metaphysics, science and technology. Strong rationality is not achieved; strong rationality is when the application of reason to tasks is assessed by some standard, including the standard of accomplishing the tasks, achieving the goals. The succession of similar cults, the failure to appraise that whole approach to goal-achievement, signals a failure to discover rationality. Why bother to make this point, which can easily lend itself to misunderstanding? Well, the answer is compassion, taking other people's problems seriously: cargo cults are not ivory-tower abstractions. They display much distressed behaviour, much futile organizational effort and sometimes result in serious destruction of wealth

47

and supplies. So their intellectual errors, their rational deficiency, have grave consequences that one would like to help avoid.

By contrast, rain dances probably do no harm, so they are not counter-productive (unless for example they consume energy and resources that might better be spent digging wells) and hence can do little harm; but they also can do little good either. Rain does not respond to human wishes, or the will of non-existent gods and spirits. Rain is a meteorological phenomenon reflecting simple chemical and physical processes of the water cycle but worked over by so many variables as to be almost unpredictably complex in detail, and dependent upon forces so vast and diffused as to be very little under human control at all. Irrigation and flood control, storing water, getting it from other sources, these are the sorts of actions we would commend as strongly rational in the situation. So with cargo cultists.

If it is canned goods, flashlights and jeeps that cargo cultists want to acquire they can either enter the money economy and so bargain their goods and services for them, or they can act to create a manufacturing economy of their own. If it is the social status and political power they associate with these goods that they really want still other courses of action need to be under-taken. Either way, they need to strengthen their own rationality – how they apply reason to tasks. Their traditional stock of beliefs about the spirit-origins of the cargo may be retained, but not as basic for action, since by no standard, however weak, do they inspire successful completion of the tasks of acquiring goods or socio-political status. A minimum standard of rationality is to abandon lines of approach that repeatedly fail. Cargo-cult experi-ence can improve rationality as much as explanatory ideas. Cultists can learn from experience, act more effectively as a result, and learn to learn from experience how better to learn from experi-ence, i.e. how to improve their rationality from weak to strong.[17]

1.9 Weak and strong rationality

In our influential theoretical paper on this whole question, Agassi and I (1967) identified rationality with acting to achieve ends and ranked three kinds of rationality according to the extent that they displayed learning from experience. Rationality$_0$, we thought, was action directed towards some end and predicated on some body of ideas and information. Cargo cults and rain dances were rational$_0$. Rationality$_1$ was goal-directed action based on the best ideas and information according to some explicit standard. Rationality$_2$, one our commentators have struggled to understand, is the notion expounded on in his monograph, namely goal-directed action employing the best ideas and information as assessed not by some standard or other but by the best standard. What does it mean, 'the best standard'? Well, some philosophers might argue that the best ideas and information are those gained by induction from experience. But the method of induction is a fraud, so we find that standard wanting. Other philosophers think a combination of ideas and information is to be judged by its capacity to predict. We think that known-to-be-false systems can be excellent predictors. At all events we think these standards of assessment should be discussed and we declared openly that we thought Popper's philosophy science was the best standard yet available for assessing a body of ideas or information.

Applying our ideas you could say that cargo-cult activity displayed not so much irrationality as weak rationality or call it rationality$_0$, because it was based on the best information available in the culture but not on the best information period. It just so happens that for a host of reasons the best information was not available to that culture.

This brings out very clearly that rationality, tied as it is to learning from experience, is in turn tied to assessing learning from experience. There must be experience to help learn and a world to learn about and some notion of improvement or progress in that learning, some notion of truth and error, so assessment of effectiveness of means, for there to be strong rationality. Such a view is inimical to cognitive relativism, as we shall see.

This in turn explains why magic, science and religion seem to lie at the heart of debates about rationality. Why Peter Winch's much-discussed paper (1964) is a commentary on Sir Edward Evans-Pritchard's brilliant study of *Witchcraft, Oracles and Magic Among the Azande*. Why W. R. G. (Robin) Horton's widely discussed papers start from his studies of the religious world-view of the Kalabari tribe in Nigeria, one he had studied closely and whose features he enjoys comparing to western science and cosmology (Horton 1964, 1967a and b, 1973a, 1973b, 1975, 1976a, 1976b, 1979, 1982). It is human thought, our cognitive efforts, that clearly demand assessment if rationality has to do with learning from experience, because, as Tylor and Frazer argued, magic, religion and science are all systems of thought that reflect the emerging effort to learn from experience, to understand the world, to construct pictures of the way things are.

This neo-Frazerian attribution of rationality, i.e. learning from experience by conjecture and refutation, to almost everyone, annoyed neo-Durkheimians no end, not to mention those immovably convinced that religious thinking and hence religious belief are totally unlike scientific or rational or empirical thinking and scientific belief. At the very least, it was suggested, science is an instrumental modality, its idea is to manipulate the world, whereas religion is about higher things. I remain unconvinced. And a vigorous debate with J. H. M. Beattie over our magic paper shows (Beattie 1964, 1966; Jarvie and Agassi 1967; Beattie 1970; Jarvie and Agassi 1973) that the other side, particularly the symbolists, such as Needham, Beattie and Leach, are quite unconvinced too.

> And what is done, in cargo cults as in Ghost Dances and in other comparable social change rituals, is to enact, through a variety of symbolic performances, a kind of ritual drama. Essentially, cargo cults provide something to do, not just something to think, although of course they do that too. They do not seem to me to be primarily, as Jarvie suggests, types of explanatory theory; rather they are recourses, in times of stress, to the consolations of rite and drama; in a very fundamental sense to the consolations of make-believe. (Beattie 1966, p. 71)

Why downplay cargo cults as something to think? Because belief does not explain action, they maintain, and to say that it does is to commit the fallacy of intellectualism. Christians in general may believe the same things yet act very differently; magicians may act much the same yet have idiosyncratically different beliefs. Intellectualism is such a dirty word in anthropology, the caricature of it as the if-I-were-a horse argument so ingrained,[18] that it is very hard to get over the idea that anti-intellectualism rests on a grasp of science and of thinking that needs to be rectified in order for rehabilitated intellectualism to be confronted. There is no rational thinking as such; there is simply problem-solving as best as we can, which is a sub-category of goal-directed or rational action.

1.10 Further problems with cognitive interpretations

Another reason why cognitive systems raise especially acute problems for the doctrine of the rational unity of mankind is because those systems may include denials of it. They may, for example, deny the basic canons of rationality, such as the necessity to avoid and to eliminate contradictions in our ideas; they may claim that the only true knowledge is religious or mystical enlightenment and further claim that that is already given to us in dogma or present only to those who open themselves to the experience; they may even explicitly divide the world into rational and civilized men and irrational and uncivilized savages, as the Ancient Greeks did. Obviously, then, the diversity of cognitive systems is a grave problem for the rational unity of mankind.

My own view is that mankind's capacity to act rationally, to pursue goals, to learn from experience, is unique to this particular species of animal and that science is the paradigm case of rationality as learning from experience. It is therefore important to overcome the difficulties I have outlined. This can be done, while allowing degrees of rationality to alternative cognitive systems and allowing full rationality to actions based upon those cognitive systems. Thinking, believing and acting are all, I have been arguing, to be subsumed under the same model of rationality, namely that of goal-directed or aim-orientated action.

I have already set aside the endlessly heard objection that there is more to magic and religion than their cognitive content (emotions; symbolism); or even that if there is any cognitive content (which some would deny) it is sociologically insignificant. This may be true and for the sake of my argument I shall grant it, even though I myself think cognitive content is here of paramount importance. All I need for my argument is agreement that there does appear to be *some* putative cognitive content in the thought-systems we call magic and religion.

Let me also set aside the worry that the three categories, magic, religion and science, are not distinct and hence should not be treated as though they were. As a disciple of Tylor and Frazer, who saw an evolutionary connection between them, I can hardly operate with some hard-and-fast distinction. Not being an evolutionist, I can go even further and say I believe there are elements of the other two in each of the three. There are strong magical and religious elements in science, both content and practice; and the same goes for magic and for religion. The labels are simply analytical distinctions best employed in the manner suggested by Frazer. This rough and ready distinction turns on whether the causal agents thought to be at work are manipulable animated natural forces, in which case we call it 'magic'; personalized supernatural forces, in which case we call it 'religion'; or impersonal, inanimate natural forces, in which case we call it 'science'. Where there is a mix or an overlap the label we choose will depend on the purpose at hand – hence such coinages as 'magico-religious' systems of thought.

1.11 Views of science

Much of the strength of my discussion draws upon a non-traditional notion of science. Deriving mainly from Popper, but reflecting also the impact of Agassi and Gellner, I offer a quite broad picture of science, one in which it merges back imperceptibly into myth and story. On the methodological level I follow Popper in identifying science with the impulse to learn from experience by confronting experience, by challenging it with theories, myths, ideas, conjectures and guesses, and by responding to difficulties in doing this by viewing them as learning experiences. Hence empiricism, inductivism, indeed all claims to a special method above and beyond that involving an attitude of learning and a procedure of trial and error, I consider too narrowing a picture of science. But in holding up science as an embodiment of the strongest idea of rationality (rationality$_2$), one has to take into account the historical context that colours the reactions of most of one's readers. For traditionally the rationality of science has been identified with far more precise methods and procedures than the truisms of trial and error, and as specifically hostile to all sorts of things (such as myth and story) my view is not in the least hostile to. For example many humanists of the present generation identify science with cold and anti-life objectivity (cf. the Lawrence v. Russell debate mentioned earlier), with a false detachment of subject from object (phenomenology); with mechanism (Marxists); with a denial of mystery (mystics); with positivism (whatever that now can mean); and so on. I want not to be saddled with any of these attributions, although I cannot expend space endlessly explaining what I do not mean or intend or imply. I know that whatever I say I am going to be read as committing myself to all those things. So be it.

The key matter here is to set aside the specific historical identifications of science with certain kinds of models of rationality. One of the oldest was the identification of science with Euclidean geometry, namely an ordered and systematic set of deductions from explicit premises. Even today there are philosophers of science (not so many scientists) who think a subject hasn't finally become scientific until it is set out in a modern version of Euclid's formal system: with axioms, theorems, lemmas, derivations, etc. This picture of the rationality of science I find too strong and specific not because it rules out magic and religion (which it does not) but because it denies rationality to too much good science. There is the historical fact that science is a living tradition, a set of customs, social institutions and personnel, sets of books, papers, documents and apparatus, and a great many errors, side-tracks, complete nonsense. This is real science and this is also rational science, not some imaginary Euclidean formal system. If science is the search to find out what is written in the Book of Nature there is no good reason to think that it is written in a formal language system.

Science is also sometimes identified with the method of induction from experience, with slow and tentative advance up the ladder of inductive generalization, starting from indubitable facts and reaching indubitable axioms of experience. This too is an excessively strong and exclusionary view of rationality. Once again, my picture of science stumbling and fumbling, starting at all sorts of weird places (e.g. sun worship), setting out to legitimate prejudices, to upset the establishment, gain the Nobel Prize, proceeding intuitively, getting stuck, jumping to conclusions, getting all the ideas at once in a rush, taking a lifetime looking for an idea and failing (Einstein and Unified Field Theory), and there being nothing at all resembling hard and fast facts to start all this from will not fit the inductivist strait-jacket. Our present knowledge, as we laughingly call it, is an unsystematic and probably quite unreliable chaos. It is, however, all we have and we begin from there and scramble towards where we want to get using whatever footholds and handholds we can reach, and taking the falls that result.

Furthermore, as in climbing, what looks like the way to a peak may lead down, what looks like a peak may be only a ridge, one may climb to the top only to spot a higher point further on. Indeed my picture of science is such that it cannot be identified with any too specific a system or procedure, since it is a social institution. Efforts to attribute a system or procedure to it are efforts to reform and shape it, to help it improve its own rationality, its capacity to learn from its own experience. The success of such efforts is quite moot. No one, including Popper, believes there awaits us an algorithm for the successful acquisition of knowledge, for the successful solution of problems. Hence the standing of methodological rules is problematic. Only by stressing that learning is mainly learning from mistakes do they make sense. We may devise some negative procedural rules that fence off obvious pitfalls, but these rules cannot otherwise show us the way to go.

The picture of science I offer, then, need be no stronger than this. We can learn to avoid some mistakes. This is a weak sense of progress. It gives us at best a little more power over ourselves and nature. We try to be orderly and systematic because it has the negative value of being a way of searching for mistakes, gaps, inconsistencies. Science does presuppose there is an external world that is in some sort of determinate state, i.e. in some sort of state such that when we make statements about it some of them can be mistaken – not to mention irrelevant, foolish, metaphorical, etc.

This is an image of science that somewhat transcends its embodiments in actual scientists and actual social institutions. It is normative and descriptive, because it is at the heart of science that it strives to better its content and its procedures. Hence it is descriptively constituted by its own norms. It is an image of science that lends some objectivity to our thinking, to our cognitive efforts. But it is an extremely liberal – I should say radical – view of the scientific enterprise. It is a picture of science that does not exclude magic, does not exclude religion and does not exclude emotion, feeling, superstition, darkness, the aesthetic, and so on. But it is a picture that denies the attempt to characterize primitive man as without science and also denies the picture of primitive man as somehow thinking in a manner that is totally different, more primitive or whatever and that in order to do science and become rational he needs to rectify his thought processes.

1.12 Rationality as rational thinking

Now that it is clear that I want rationality to be taken socially, as a characteristic of social systems, namely as a classification of the arrangements for learning from experience, I am in a position to tackle directly the alternative – rationality as mental act rather than social act. Two clearly related mental acts are involved: *thought* and *belief*. Thought is a process, belief an outcome. The two are connected. The outcome of some thought processes is the establishment of beliefs. Some would say rational = belief arrived at by rational thought processes (such as induction from experience); others would say thinking rationally about a topic means having rational beliefs about it (involving only observables, e.g.). But we need not accept these stipulations. Let us explore them separately. This matter of *rational thinking*.

Western culture is permeated with the idea that there is a split in the nature of man between thinking and feeling, reason and emotion, the rational and the irrational; the one side is cool, calculating, detached and reasonable; the other, warm, impulsive, involved and unreasonable. Life is sometimes depicted as a struggle between these two sides: emotion causes you to fall in love, but reason should decide whether to marry. Emotions lead us to war, reason is required to make peace. Perhaps our follies come from emotion, our successes from reason. Perhaps. Romantics and the followers of 'blood and soil' think otherwise. Rationalists always felt that the danger was, as Hume put it, that reason is and always will be the slave of the passions.

In late nineteenth-century evolutionist anthropology this split emerges in the view of human history as the evolutionary triumph of reason, or rational thinking, which has led to enlightenment, science, industry, progress and High Victorianism (I apologize for the irony) over the dark forces of ignorance, superstition, contagion, association, emotion, mysticism and primitive fear. Primitive societies were those dominated by magic, taboo and even religion and hence prone to those sentiments. The hope for salvation lay in their grasp of rudimentary technology which could be built on and their contact with 'civilization' which would do the building necessary to bring them up into the light. Enlightenment was science, industrial technology and the Church of England. Passion, then, is dark and primitive; where life is governed by these forces of primitive mentality, we get primitive culture. What was this non-rational thinking like?

Two main views of in what primitive thinking consisted contended. Lévy-Bruhl thought that it was 'pre-logical' – *logic* was the measure of rationality. Tylor and Frazer thought *science* was the measure of rationality and for them = empiricism and induction. Hence while Lévy-Bruhl saw a shift of balance from the complete dominance of mystical thinking in primitive society to its subordination to logical thinking in modern society, even though mystical thinking would always be with us, Tylor and Frazer saw empiricism and its product science as a progressive force that would vanquish the forces of unreason altogether. They drew the subtle consequence that magic was less irrational than religion because it was more empirical.

The bifurcated model of the mind that associates science with its rational, i.e. non-emotional, side is matched in popularity by the model that there are different kinds of thinking and that science stems from one kind only. The modern exponent of this view is Lucien Lévy-Bruhl in his *Les Fonctions mentales dans les sociétés inférieurs* of 1910. Lévy-Bruhl demarcates primitive thinking from logical or modern thinking and he places these on a time scale: primitive thinking is earlier, logical thinking later. He does not hold that logical thinking extirpates primitive thinking, merely that it becomes dominant.[19]

How we think, according to Lévy-Bruhl, has to do with how we participate in society. Primitive society is small-scale, undifferentiated, and each person plays many roles: familial, political, judicial, religious, economic. In primitive society people participate in the whole, in their thinking as well as their doing; that thinking is mystical and prelogical: participatory. Mystical thinking resorts to explanation involving forces, influences and actions that are imperceptible (p. 33). Pre-logical thinking is that which does not bind itself down as modern thought does, to avoiding contradiction. Instead it is unspecific about what connections can be made, things are what they are and something else as well. 'The dictum deduced from Hume's argument, that "anything may produce anything," might have served as a motto for primitive mentality' (338). As the social group grows and differentiates, as the division of labour spreads, the holistic participation is spoiled, allowing logical thinking, objective classification and perception to emerge.

Lévy-Bruhl is a thinker who has been much misunderstood, caricatured, even vilified. The problems of interpreting him are compounded by his own shifts of view and qualification within a rather large corpus of writings. His stoutest defender was Evans-Pritchard who in his 1934 article and in his posthumous 1981 history of the field, commends Lévy-Bruhl's work for its thought-provoking quality. And indeed we can see the sources of his own epoch-making ideas of 1937 already present:

> savages are prevented from pursuing enquiries into the workings of nature by their collective representations. These formalised patterns of thought, feeling, and behaviour, inhibit any cognitive, affective, or motor, activities which conflict with them. (1934, p. 41)

After correcting us about Lévy-Bruhl on the savage dislike of discursive thought:

> It is due neither to incapacity nor inaptitude, since those who have drawn our attention to this feature of primitive mentality expressly state that among them are 'minds quite as capable of scientific thought as those of Europeans' . . . Neither is it the result of profound intellectual torpor, of enervation . . . for these same natives . . . show themselves . . . observant, wise, skilful, clever, even subtle, when an object interests them. (Lévy-Bruhl 1922, pp. 29–30)

the question arises of what Evans-Pritchard thinks Lévy-Bruhl does mean:

> If the mystical thought of a savage is socially determined so also is the scientific thought of a civilized person. Therefore, any evaluation between the savage's capacity for 'logical thinking' and the civilized man's capacity for 'logical thinking' is irrelevant to the question at issue which is whether patterns of thought are orientated mystically in primitive societies and orientated scientifically in civilized societies . . . are both thinking in patterns of thought provided for us by the societies in which we live. (Evans-Pritchard 1934, pp. 48–9)

There is no 'mystical thinking', there are collective representations, i.e. social models. When a man is killed by a spear-thrust the savage works vengeance with magic, directed against the other's magic and its perpetrator (We after all, blame he who spears, not the spear.) Everyone can think, says Evans-Pritchard, but not everyone's thinking obeys the canons of logic and scientific method. This is what is missing. He seems to want to detach the psychologism, to talk not of people's thinking, but of the social institutions of logic and scientific method, so yielding a distinction, a non-invidious and valid distinction, much like the way we distinguish between acephalous and other societies, between matrilineal and patrilineal societies, between those with totems and those without.

Returning to Lévy-Bruhl thirty years later, Evans-Pritchard was more inclined to accept that society does contain different ways of thinking:

> Lévy-Bruhl could have posed the problem to better advantage. It is not so much a question of primitive versus civilized mentality as the relation of two types of thought to each other in any society . . . a problem of levels of thought and experience . . . Had he not been so positivistic . . . he might have asked himself . . . what are the functions of the two kinds of thought in any society . . . the kinds associated with what are sometimes distinguished as the 'expressive' and the 'instrumental'. (1965, pp. 91–2)

How very different were the views of the English School of Tylor and Frazer on the same issues. For them rationality was to be equated not with logic but with empiricism, and empiricism was equated with science. French logic led to failed Cartesian physics, English empiricism led to Newton. Magic, Tylor and Frazer noted, engaged in prediction and experimentation. Its failures led its followers to mysticism and religion, and the failure of those, in turn, led to a revival of empiricism and hence science. Although this view of magic is resisted in some quarters, I will quote a field anthropologist:

> Behind this ritual idiom there stands a most rigid and never-questioned dogma, learnt by every child in infancy and forced home by countless instances of everyday usage based upon it and meaningless without it or in its despite. This dogma, in general, is that effects are secured by incantation and that without incantation such effects cannot come to pass . . . In brief, there is no natural theory of yam growth, of the powers of canoe lashings, of fish nets, of gift exchange in strange places overseas, of disease and death, of wind and rain, of love between man and woman. All these things cannot possibly exist in their own right. All are supernaturally created

57

by the ritual incantation with the help of the appropriate technological processes in agriculture, canoe-making, fishing preparation and with the help of more mundane wooing in overseas gift-exchange and in love-making, but without any such extra work in making wind and rain, disease and death or in their counteracting (apart only from the practice of bleeding the patient in some cases of illness). This latter type of unaided incantation expresses truly the attitude of the native towards incantation throughout. It is the really important factor in producing an effect. (Fortune 1932, pp. 97–8)

Philosophers, of all people, are responsible for discovering the decisive arguments that refute both identifications – that of rational thought with the logical and that of rational thought with the empirical. Sir Francis Bacon formulated the argument about logic in the early seventeenth century. He pointed to the well-known fact that what any valid syllogism does is simply re-arrange the pattern of the terms, it does not add anything new. There is nothing in the conclusion that is not already contained in the premisses.[20] But the rational endeavour of science is to get new knowledge, so logic cannot be the basis of its rationality. In the late nineteenth century two logicians especially, Husserl and Frege, added the point that logic is not the study of correct (subjective) thought processes at all, but the study of correct (objective) patterns of argument and hence is no more about mentality than is mathematics, which is the (objective) study of the necessary properties of different worlds.

Some have concluded from this that logic has nothing to do with rationality, or that science is not rational. I hardly think this is warranted. The correct conclusion is that whatever rational thinking is, it is not a psychological state. But it would, for example, not be rational to violate the law of contradiction – I think it is easy to show that that would be inimical to learning from experience.

As to the argument identifying rational thought with science, with empiricism and induction, David Hume, a great rationalist, found two great difficulties here. The first is that science is the knowledge of causes, whereas empiricism is a doctrine of what can be experienced through the senses; the second is, how do we get from facts to causes? Hume says you can see objects but you can't see causes. He then says, define cause as simply one observable event being constantly followed by ('conjoined with') another. But then, he says, how can we know of it? No matter how many times we have seen it, next time things could be different. No, you reply, because the course of nature does not change. How do we know that, he answers, only because you have always seen that it is so. Next time it could be different, because you can never *see* anything that will make it necessarily so.

To those who simply abandon a science of causes Hume would have answered that science was knowledge of causes because a causeless universe does not obey the principle of sufficient reason (things are the way they are for a reason and change only for a reason). Such a universe is not rational and cannot support an ordered science.

The breakdown of the attempts to link rational thought to logic or to empiricism may have been discovered by philosophers, but the despair it evokes goes well beyond that group of specialists. The two arguments feed a despair of reason and provide excuses for three characteristic irrationalist and anti-rationalist reactions: they are dogmatism, scepticism and mysticism. All three are used as stepping stones to the relativism we shall discuss in Part Two.

Dogmatism is the continued re-iteration of a failed idea as though repeated saying makes it so. Even today we can hear assertions to the effect that attention to the facts, or to the senses, or to logic is the measure of rational thought. Residual positivism is often in the background. Dogmatism on such issues is, however, the antithesis of rational thought.

Scepticism is despair not of this or that idea, but of the hope itself that human thought can find answers. Hume himself is classified as a sceptic because at certain points he seems to think that balanced arguments can be found on both sides of most points (such as whether rational thought leads to science) and hence that decisions have to be handed over to common sense, tradition or inclination.

Mysticism is the despair less of thought than of articulation. The mystic believes in truth or enlightenment but does not think rational methods, whether logical, empirical or other, are the path to follow. Instead some combination of faith and practice will do it, but only for each individual singly. No general articulable knowledge results.

In so far as the search for rationality is a search for the principle unifying mankind, the collapse of that version that explicates rationality as rational thought is a blow to that project. The three irrational reactions, dogmatism, scepticism and mysticism, can be used to argue that mankind is unified only in its diversity and that no principle exists to explain and sort out that diversity. This is one formulation of relativism which I shall try to show is not compatible with the doctrine of the unity of mankind.

1.13 Rationality as rational belief

Now to rational belief. Or rather the identification of human rationality, the unifying principle of humanity, with the holding of rational beliefs. What would rational belief be? A rational *doctrine*? A rational belief *is* a rational doctrine. What is a rational doctrine? Science? That's rather broad. Axiomatized thermodynamics? That's rather narrow. Euclid's *Elements*? Only science and mathematics? The thirty-nine articles of the Church of England? Astrology? How do we discriminate among such candidates? Again: what is rational *belief in* a given doctrine – believing the right things for the right reasons? What would such reasons be like?

The demarcation of rational beliefs and the identification of the right reasons coincide in the philosophy of empiricism: the right beliefs are those based on observation (your 'own or trusted others'), observation is the right reason for believing them. The paradigm of this observationalist empiricism is science. All it commands any human being to do is 'Open your eyes and see'. The great attraction of empiricism is its common sense, its simplicity, its optimism (problems will be solved by opening our eyes), and its egalitarianism – all of us can observe, all of us can be rational and orderly in our thinking, all of us can be scientists. A beautiful scheme. What a pity we have to muddy the picture. But, as we have seen, empiricism breaks down, induction breaks down, realism itself if taken too naively breaks down because clearly science and mathematics sometimes dabble in things that are anything but real, e.g. non-Euclidean geometry.

To recap. Rational belief means there are certain doctrines or ideas that are themselves the touchstones of a person's rationality. This has in the past been held of religion. Nowadays it is more commonly held of common sense, or of Marxism or of science. Whatever the candidate the problem is the same: beliefs change and doctrines change. What is a rational belief at one time can have one burned at the stake, sent to the Gulag Archipelago, or ridiculed at another time.

Such a realization can lead to the same sort of breakdown and despair as we found with rational thought. The three characteristic reactions of dogmatically affirming some beliefs as rational, sceptically concluding that none are, or mystically holding that they surpass understanding, emerge once again. Some anthropologists measure cargo cultists' ideas against current science and find them rationally wanting. Others maintain that what is rational belief for us is not for cargo cultists. And Edward Rice (1974) has implied that he is prepared to grant that it is rational for cultists on Tanna to maintain that they have made spirit journeys and communed with the spirit of the dead prophet John Frum even if such mysteries are closed to the white man.

> Westerners must try to accept Cargo on its own terms, not theirs, for Cargo is a reality, even though their western-conditioned minds tell them it is impossible . . . (Rice 1974, p. xv).

Such despair of reason is excessive but entirely characteristic. It results from excessive expectations. Whence these expectations? Well, the discovery, in Ancient Greece, of what we call mathematics and its exemplary character as an achievement of reason led to the question of, if in mathematics, why not elsewhere? When modern science appears on the scene, employing mathematics and achieving spectacular success, a clear polarity develops.

We see mathematics and science as rational (even the irrationalists agree), mysticism and superstition as irrational. Where do we draw the line of demarcation? Here we can turn to Popper's demarcation based on attitude to error: the difference lies in the attitude of learning from it. In Bartley's (1968) formulation the stress is even more on sociological features, because he is concerned to show that some systems of ideas have built-in evasion strategies to avoid learning from experience, and these are the pillars of intellectual irrationalism, sharply to be demarcated from open-minded learning systems.

So we get the answer that rational belief is belief held in an open-minded, critical manner: no set of ideas is rational, rationality inheres rather in the manner in which they are held. Rationality is, then, different from truth. True beliefs are not the same as rational beliefs. It is entirely possible to entertain in an irrational manner statements that are true, namely by adopting a dogmatic or otherwise uncritical stance towards them. It is entirely possible to entertain in a rational manner statements that are false, namely by adopting a critical attitude towards them.

1.14 Science as the supreme embodiment of rationality

In Evans-Pritchard (1937), we can find the suggestion to identify rationality neither with logic (although that is part of it) nor with empiricism (although that is part too) but with features of the social and cognitive systems to which we belong. A system subject to self-conscious review, both as a system and as to its adequacy, hence to criticism and to change, is more rational than one without these features. This is argued apropos the closed and defensive thought system of the Azande. A most remarkably prescient book. The book outlines a weird and fascinating culture permeated by witchcraft (bad) and magic (good) and sorcery (both). It shows how it all fits neatly together as Evans-Pritchard even tested the oracle for some of his own decisions and it worked quite well.

> I never found great difficulty in observing oracle consultations.
> I found that in such matters the best way of gaining
> confidence was to enact the same procedure as Azande and
> to take oracular verdicts as seriously as they take them. I
> always kept a supply of poison for the use of my household
> and neighbours and we regulated our affairs in accordance
> with the oracles' decisions. I may remark that I found this as
> satisfactory a way of running my home and affairs as any
> other I know of. (1937, pp. 269–70)

For every failure there are excuses.

We can derive inspiration from Evans-Pritchard for a characterization of what it is about our social system that makes it host to science. We can suggest its rationality has to do with criticism and change. Parts of our social/cognitive system are as it were open to change and development; they do not, as Gellner stresses, collapse when some key cognitive component is replaced. The system flexibly incorporates and adapts to change of ideas, rather than resorting to ad hoc defences, still less to mystical, dogmatic or sceptical despair. As Evans-Pritchard says, in a closed system 'the web [of belief] is not an external structure in which he is enclosed. It is the texture of his thought and he cannot think that his thought is wrong' (Evans-Pritchard 1937, p. 195). If Evans-Pritchard is right here, the very difficult problem is how do savage societies ever learn, ever make the transition to open and changing ones? How did it happen historically, how does it happen now? How is what Gellner calls the Big Ditch between the savage and the modern mind crossed?

Those who would say the savage never enters into the modern thought-system have to say we or our predecessors were never savages. If the transition ever happens, and I suppose it must have, doubtless it is a partial, piecemeal, haphazard process. One explanation of it ever happening might be that a teacher somewhere once challenged his students to criticize and improve on his ideas. Why would he do that? Was he a saint? Perhaps it was culture clash, his familiarity with alternative ideas, perhaps awareness that other peoples acted and believed differently with apparent reason (rationality); the very sort of realization about

Azande magic that led Evans-Pritchard to assert that it was as rational a way to conduct everyday affairs as any other. Not as much as science, perhaps, but then we don't employ science to govern all our everyday affairs. Perhaps it was just a reckless challenge that was surprisingly fruitful and stimulating. Thus is acquired or invented the social embodiment of open-mindedness. Thought process and actual beliefs are no mark of rationality.

So rational *thinking* is problem- or goal-orientated thinking and results in rational beliefs only if they are held open to criticism; and rational action is simply a model that embraces both. Science is a paradigm of rationality not because of its ideas, not because it is true; not because it is the result of special kinds of social institutions that foster if they do not impose the critical and open-minded attitude of wanting to learn from experience. These institutions include language, traditions of argument, libraries, universities, journals, seminars, laboratories, conferences, and so on. Despite all these institutions science falls short of the norms it endeavours to embody. We can find there dogmatism, both personal and institutional; mysticism, mainly personal; thought-control, propaganda, careerism, corruption and so on. Yet, like democracy, a terrible system but the best we have, science remains the best approach to rationality we have. The forces of irrationality and corruption are strong and have constantly to be struggled against: all social institutions require constant surveillance, maintenance, repair and improvement.

The rational unity of mankind, then, is less an article of belief and more a social programme (based, no doubt, on moral conviction) under which we attempt to construct a certain sort of community of men in which we face openly and unsparingly the necessity and value of learning from experience, articulating our problems and assessing our solutions and hoping that in the process we make some modest progress in alleviating the worst features of our environment and of our lives together.

Part two

Relativism

He that will carefully peruse the history of mankind and look abroad into the several tribes of men, and with indifferency survey their actions, will be able to satisfy himself, that there is scarce that principle of morality to be named, or rule of virtue to be thought on (those only excepted that are absolutely necessary to hold society together, which commonly too are neglected betwixt distinct societies), which is not, somewhere or other, slighted and condemned by the general fashion of whole societies of men, governed by practical opinions and rules of living quite opposite to others.

Locke, *Essay*, Book I, 3, 10

2.1 Relativism, moral and cognitive

The problem of relativism is the problem of sustaining the principle of the moral unity of mankind in the face of the vast diversity of man's moral practices. The moral unity of mankind is the idea that all men are of equal moral worth – a sentiment that can be cashed out in a host of ways. It can mean men are entitled to equal moral treatment. It can mean men agree on their moral prescriptions and proscriptions. It can mean that the human race constitutes a single universe of moral discourse in which there must be some universal moral principles. It can mean that the notion of morality is found everywhere. Whatever the interpretation, it is contentious. There is not universal agreement that all men are entitled to equal moral treatment. In one society or another we can find race, rank, standing, wealth, power, moral condition and degree of ritual purity all affecting moral treatment. As Locke noted in the motto, there is scarce a principle of morality or a rule of virtue that is not slighted and condemned by the practices of other societies. Savages were arguably part of the human race but it was long thought they had no morality and hence did not participate in the universe of discourse (see the discussion of the Amerindians in § 1.7 above).

The most glaring and problematic contradiction, however, is found in opposition to the general formulation: many societies would concede that slaves, women and children are members of the human race, but would not concede their equal moral worth and hence entitlement to equal moral treatment. As property they receive their moral standing from, and treatment only at the whim of, their owners.

Relativism seems to come about like this. Assume all men are of equal moral worth. This seems to imply that what they do is of equal moral worth: in thought and deed, in their judgments of value and of truth, their construction of intellectual, valuational, technical and social structures. Hence if one culture excoriates all others, words and deeds, as worthy only of destruction, dispersal and enslavement, there is no way, without violating the principle of equal moral worth, that such excoriation can be criticized. It looks as though cultures have to beg to differ. One culture believes other people are not human beings and so not of equal moral worth, another believes women and children are men's property and property has no inherent moral worth or moral rights, still another believes that equal moral worth is achieved, not inherent, still another that it is ascribed to some, achieved by others but not by everyone, and so on.

By what argument can those who propose equal moral worth defeat these alternatives and establish their own? It looks hopeless. But perhaps here is a chink in this seemingly headlong clash: examination of each unit, culture or society, for *consistency*. If we can detect inconsistencies in the articulated or implicit views of a culture, we may then argue that not all of what is being maintained can be maintained together. Then we may suggest evidential and consequentialist tests for sifting the views. Obviously, where views are not articulated or are embodied in practices[1] little can be done.

The problem of rationality was to a certain extent a conceptual problem. A conceptual problem arises when a word – rationality – is employed by many different commonsense and philosophical theories and confusion can only be cleared up by criticizing those theories and settling on a theory that explains and permits these others to make sense. The problem of relativism is rather more of a theoretical and practical problem, less a problem of confusion needing clarification, more one of error and inconsistency needing to be corrected, practice to be defended. Clearly, one of the great hopes of mankind is that there is a species unity of interests and hence of mutual regard, that will sooner or later win out over the forces of divisiveness, partiality, parochialism, and domination that currently set us apart from one another. But before I go any further with this, I must clear up something that may bother the tidy-minded reader.

Relativism comes in several packages, the most general is cultural relativism; this is conventionally divided into cognitive relativism and moral relativism. I have decided for purposes of symmetry in this book to treat of moral/cultural relativism in this part. Cognitive relativism strikes me as rather different from moral relativism, although they are sometimes treated alike. Moral diversity stimulates moral relativism. However, the diversity of human cognitive efforts is not the sole buttress to cognitive relativism. There is as well an argument at a meta-level that goes to suggest that all cognition, in some way or other, is suspect. Let me illustrate with cargo cults once more.

Cargo cults, like all religions, contain conjectures about the make-up of the world and what we human beings can do to make things happen in it. These conjectures have great charm and beauty. Here are two of my favourites:
A cargo prayer:

> O Father Consel, you are sorry for us. You can help us. We have nothing – no aircraft, no ships, no jeeps, nothing at all. The Europeans steal it from us. You will be sorry for us and send us something. (Lawrence 1954)

And an idea of how the cults catch up with current affairs:

> in 1964 . . . a tribe in New Hanover had refused to pay its taxes and, instead, had saved up all of its money to 'buy' President Lyndon Johnson. By getting 'numbah-one man belong America' into their camp, the natives of Kavieng and other villages in New Hanover were sure they would be able to get their hands on the white man's goods. A native prophet predicted that the *Queen Mary* would arrive on June sixteenth, and would disgorge 600 black-American troops, who would 'liberate us from the Australian oppressors.' . . . soon at least 2,500 of the island's 7,000 or so natives were firm believers in the Messiah from the Pedernales . . . the handsome young prophet of the Johnson Cult . . . asked Healy [an Australian official] if he would do a favor for the people of the village. He handed over a heavy bag containing more than $1,000 in shilling pieces. The money, Bos Mailik explained, was what they had gathered to 'buy' President Johnson. Would Healy handle the transaction for them? (Machlin 1970, pp. 24–5)

Some are rather vague, some are metaphysical and some are clear, precise and false. False? Yes, just that. It is quite fair to say something like this. To the extent that the cults endeavour to reunite the living with their dead ancestors, so far as can be known nothing we can do will bring this goal nearer. Compare the dreadful story of eleven-year-old Wesley Parker of Barstow, California, a diabetic, whose parents took him to a faith healer to be cured, then threw out his insulin supply. Within two days the boy was seriously ill, but his father concluded, 'I knew then that the diabetes was caused by two demons and that we could no longer give him insulin without inviting the demon back.' The demons were commanded to leave the boy's body, but he died anyway. The father refused burial because he was sure his son would be resurrected. At a prayer meeting the boy was commanded to rise from the dead, but he lay still in his casket. Even after the funeral the father maintained he had misinterpreted God's word and that his son would rise from the dead four days after he was buried, as in the Biblical story of Lazarus (UPI report in *Honolulu Advertiser*, August 1978).

To the extent that the cults endeavour to bring about concrete social changes such as increased wealth for Melanesians, an end to discrimination and exploitation, and entry into the modern world with all its benefits and shortcomings, they propose costly, wasteful and ineffective methods. Prayer, religious organization, ritual purification, demonstrations of faith are not going to accomplish these goals.[2]

Concentrating then on such accomplishable goals, I want to make the case that not all approaches are relativistically equal. The goals may be achieved, but not by means of cargo-cult activity. On the basis of a scientific picture of the world and a social scientific picture of how people can make things happen we can I think extend a hopeful alternative to the Melanesians. Cashcrops, industrialization, appropriate reorganization of society along bureaucratic-rational lines, these are a better recipe for achieving the goals. Making no judgment on the goals (although I believe that can be done too, see Gellner 1973b, 1975, 1980, 1983), I nevertheless bring the rationality discussed in Part I to oppose the relativism to be discussed in Part II.

Offering scientific rationality as an alternative to cargo cults would hardly seem sufficient to defeat relativism, but it is. For relativism has a weak and negative case. It gains all its plausibility not from any strengths of its own (it is not usually shown to have any), but from seemingly fatal weaknesses its proponents seek out in absolutism (which is taken to be the alternative). If the alternative can be shown not to have those weaknesses, or to have weaknesses that are not fatal, then the main argumentative prop of relativism ('What's the alternative?') is removed. It then becomes possible to counter-attack and show how vague, inconsistent and defenceless relativism is.

We can counterpose science, understood as a set of social institutions embodying and guarding the tradition of critical discussion, with relativism, the doctrine that categorical judgments about such things as the falsity of cargo cults cannot be made. When I wrote above that cargo cults were false what this means to relativists is that in the context of *my* cultural criteria of falseness cargo cults are false. But in the context of cargo-cult cultural criteria of falseness they are not. And between my cultural criteria of falseness and cargo-cult cultural criteria of falseness there is no mediator.[3]

Cargo cults are a useful case because they make it vivid how this line of undermining can be turned aside. First, like many religions, cargo cults do make factual assertions and concrete predictions. We can invite ourselves to assess these by the usual means. In the event that they are false: a mountain does not open up, a ship bearing cargo and the spirits of the dead does not arrive,

> PORT MORESBY, New Guinea – Pulling the magic corks from the mountain peak didn't produce the expected torrent of riches, but New Guinea's cargo cultists keep hoping.
>
> They thought two concrete survey markers atop Mount Turu were placed there by government agents to bottle up the mountain's wealth, so 4,000 chanting cultists dug up the markers last July.
>
> Nothing happened. Now they plan to erect a $20,000 monument in Canberra and invite Queen Elizabeth and Pope Paul to attend its dedication. They feel this will assure a flood of foreign goods to their island.
> *Kitchener-Waterloo Record*, 20.10.71[4]

then we can, if the inferences to these predictions were validly drawn, work back towards the thought that some of the animating doctrines are false. Which ones are false, is, of course, problematic. But that the set is collectively false is enough to avoid a relativistic head-shaking, or a mystical gaze, or an ad hoc suggestion that perhaps they should be taken symbolically. Second, we also scrutinize cargo-cult doctrines and their implications for inconsistencies: if the way to get landing strips and jetties for the cargo transports is collective physical work, why is not that the way to get the cargo goods themselves? If the ancestors care about their dependants, why have they allowed diversion of treasure to go on so long?

So, both empirical evidence and logic can mediate between my culture and cargo-cult culture because of course I submit my suggestions as to how cultists can achieve their aims to the same tests of evidence and logic. The most extreme, or the logically most swingeing, form of relativism thus becomes that which attempts to suggest that empirical evidence and even logic itself are culturally-bound tests and cannot mediate between their culture and cultures with other views of the empirical and the logical. These lines of attack have been overcome by colleagues, as we shall explain. But here I must stress that these meta-level arguments for cognitive relativism clash with our rationality as I have argued for it, our morality, as I shall argue for it.

In setting out to discuss moral relativism, I shall try not to cover old ground where myself and others have trod before.[5] I shall digress on some quaint historical aspects, as well as worming my way through philosophical subtleties. Throughout, I shall try to be sympathetic to relativism, to stress its insights, its valid arguments, and the salutary effect its sometimes extreme postures have had on the behaviour of others. I view it as a paradigm case of what Agassi (1963) calls an intelligent error, or an important error. Yet error it is, and, so, criticized it must be.

2.2 Herskovits on method and practice

Let me begin with modern relativism's most able and sophisticated exponent, the American anthropologist Melville J. Herskovits. He was an uncompromising and extreme cultural relativist, who upheld it in the name of a tough-minded facing of facts. He was far from limiting himself to moral relativism. The way Herskovits put it was this:

> We even approach the problem of the ultimate nature of reality itself. Cassirer holds that reality can only be experienced through the symbolism of language. Is reality, then, not defined and re-defined by the ever-varied symbolisms of the innumerable languages of mankind? (Herskovits 1973, p. 15)

But setting aside this rather big gulp, what did Herskovits mean by relativism?

> The principle of cultural relativism, briefly stated, is as follows: *Judgements are based on experience, and experience is interpreted by each individual in terms of his own enculturation.* Those who hold for the existence of fixed values will find materials in other societies that necessitate a re-investigation of their assumptions. Are there absolute moral standards, or are moral standards effective only as far as they agree with the orientations of given people at a given period of their history? (Herskovits 1973, p. 15)

Herskovits believed this principle could be applied at *philosophical, methodological* and *practical* levels (see 1973, p. 32). At the philosophical level, as in the quotation, the question is raised whether there are absolute standards. In a way this is not well formulated. Of course there are absolute moral standards,

'Cruelty is wicked', and, 'Eating people is wrong', would be examples. So that is not what Herskovits meant. By 'absolute' he seems to have meant something like 'absolutely true', 'true in the absolute (not relative) sense'. It would be hard to argue for this claim, since the mere fact that an absolute truth is denied does not render it either not absolute or not true, only controversial. Probably what Herskovits wanted to say was that there are no universally agreed upon moral truths or judgments. His thesis is about moral theory and argument at the philosophical level.

Methodology is rules of procedure, so one might cash methodological relativism out in 'as if' terms: act as if, report as if, all moral standards are based on enculturation.

Finally, practice means how we behave: respect other cultures by respecting and obeying their moral standards when you go among them (if reporting is practice then the latter subsumes methodology). Do not cross forbidden social lines, do not eat forbidden food, do not break taboos, give sacrifices to the gods, etc.

Herskovits's contention that relativism can be adopted as a philosophy, a methodology or a practice, is well taken. One can object to the philosophy of relativism while endorsing it as a methodology or a practice. To recommend as a methodological device an attitude of neutrality, to eschew treating the customs of others as 'disgusting', 'revolting' or 'savage', at least in the first instance, is quite salutary. This is not to say that later, in the course of more considered judgment, one may not reintroduce such epithets, as for example Colin Turnbull does in his examination of the Ik in *The Mountain People* (1972). This book caused something of a sensation because Turnbull portrayed a society disintegrating under dislocation and starvation, living by rules (or lack of rules) that filled the reporting anthropologist with horror. He is not the first anthropologist to be less than enamoured of his subjects, but he is the first to have confessed this candidly and at length. Some of his colleagues were anything but pleased by his candour.[6]

One heard and discounted the scuttlebut only to read with surprise an imperious piece by Fredrik Barth entitled 'Calling a Colleague to Account'. Not only was this published in *Current Anthropology*, a journal with worldwide circulation, but it was given CA* treatment, meaning it was circulated in advance to other scholars, whose comments, together with the author's reply, appeared alongside the article. So lively was the response that a second round appeared eighteen months later.

The gravamen of Barth's article was that Turnbull had no business *qua* anthropologist allowing his own emotional reactions to

73

infect his scientific work (p. 102). In particular, his conclusion that the break-up and dispersion of the Ik into surrounding areas and populations was probably for the best Barth called 'systematic culturecide'. The pompous tone wonderfully masked the total moral confusion into which relativism has plunged the anthropologists.

> . . . we cannot allow many serious mistakes in the profession
> . . . Turnbull . . . deserves . . . to be sanctioned (99–100)
> . . . fails to practice the competances and ethics of our
> discipline . . . For the hygiene of our discipline and our
> mutual instruction, I call on the Associates of CURRENT
> ANTHROPOLOGY to take a different stand, and help
> clarify the ethical and practical issues . . . (1974, p. 102).

Hardly surprising that Turnbull declined to answer.

If the harsh conditions of life push people into robbing the old and children of the food from their hands, if the values and rules the society itself once lived by are being ruined, why shouldn't the anthropologists note that some are dying off and others are wandering off to join neighbouring groups if they can and himself allow that this may be an improvement? An improvement because the surrounding societies have not had it so bad, and hence their social life continues to be fairly civilized. Barth takes methodological tolerance to absurd lengths: whatever any society chooses to do has to be acceptable to the observer otherwise he will be 'called to account'. Turnbull's compassion for individuals combined with his judgment that their social arrangements are a failure is to think culturecide and such a thoughtcrime is forbidden. To this observer of the anthropological tribe that is too much: I observe anthropologists trying to be omni-tolerant and/or neutral towards almost anything and I say they are abrogating part of their responsible humanity, which just does involve making moral judgments – however uncomfortable that may make them feel (cf. Hatch 1983).

Anthropology is only a special case here. Throughout recorded history we see men and movements arguing that part or all of their present social arrangements have been weighed in the balance and found wanting. Suggestions have ranged from mild to total social revolution, 'wiping the canvas clean'. Can Barth be unaware of this? Does he think such thought is only legitimate within one's own society? But what is one's own society? Every country has class, cultural and regional divisions that could be used to label a critic an outsider. In the world today the Soviet bloc assists violent social revolutionary movements in many countries and encourages modernization, secularization and industrialization in its clients.

The western bloc too encourages development and modernization through indigenous personnel.

True, both sides make mistakes. Perhaps Turnbull made mistakes. Barth thinks anthropology cannot afford mistakes. In my epistemology we only learn from mistakes and the fear of mistakes is not an excuse for refusal to face the reality of making judgments. Relativism cannot be used to pull back from this.

As to the practical level, one can only endorse relativism here even more heartily. Anthropologists should in practice keep their mouths shut if they don't want to be cooked and eaten, or, more likely, excluded by 'their' tribe or expelled by its government. They are after all there to learn and study, with a minimum of interference and disruption. If something affects them adversely they may well choose to keep mum. But relativism in practice has limits too. The question of whether the end of learning justifies the means of silence should not be ducked. Anthropologists are engaged in systematic dishonesty when they pretend to enter into genuine human contact with their subjects of study when all the while they are manipulating their subjects for their own purposes, not disclosing their true feelings about what they are observing and hence in their silence not only lying but also being condescending. They are assuming that their host people cannot, like adults, take adverse reaction.

But to be fair it is important to see the background to the excesses of these methodological and practical injunctions. That background is the activities of travellers, explorers, conquerors, colonial administrators and missionaries – whose depredations anthropologists so rightly deplore. In the name of God, commerce, the Queen and sometimes mere curiosity, they would often judge adversely the conduct of indigenous peoples, put sanctions on it, and attempt to introduce their own, quite alien, *mores*. Basic respect for the rights of other persons was scarcely acknowledged. The excuse was that primitivity, barbarousness or childishness had to be overcome first.

Those who are still in the state to require being taken care of by others, must be protected against their own actions as well as against external injury. For the same reason, we may leave out of consideration those backward states of society in which the race itself may be considered in its nonage. The early difficulties in the way of spontaneous progress are so great, that there is seldom any choice of means for overcoming them; and a ruler full of the spirit of improvement is warranted in the use of any expedients that will attain an end, perhaps otherwise unattainable. Despotism is a legitimate mode of government in dealing with barbarians, provided the end be their improvement, and the means justified by actually effecting that end. Liberty, as a principle, has no application to any state of things anterior to the time when mankind have become capable of being improved by free and equal discussion. Until then, there is nothing for them but implicit obedience to an Akbar or a Charlemagne, if they are so fortunate as to find one . . . (Mill 1859, p. 263)

No matter how much of a society's organization turned on a custom like head-hunting, if it offended the conqueror, it had to go. No matter if the kinship system of a society was completely different from our own, if it encouraged marriage within what Christians considered the prohibited degrees of kinship, then it had to be altered. British colonial officials went to the extent of outlawing dog meat in Hong Kong!

Missionaries, conquerors and colonizers, therefore, are responsible for much behaviour that anthropologists deplore, and rightly so. Anthropologists diagnose what they call 'ethnocentrism', the view that takes it for granted that the principles and practices of your own social or ethnic group are correct and should be used as a standard to judge the principles and practices of others. As an antidote to ethnocentrism, relativism is laudable as practice.

Although there is a logical sense in which one's theoretical interest in another society is always a function of the background from which you came, from your training and preoccupations, there is also an obvious sense in which you must strive to be open to the evidence that you come across in your scientific work. It is all-too-easy to blind oneself to countervailing evidence. Hence one has to try to moderate the tendency to see things in terms of one's theories, and look for places where that involves stretching them a bit.

The encounter between the anthropologist and an alien people is a fascinating version of this struggle to see despite conceptual blinkers, one that should not be over-simplified. Complementing the oversimplifications of the missionary who thinks he carries around God's word and anyone who thinks anything else needs conversion are the oversimplifications of the anthropologist who suggests that an attitude of respectful acceptance is owed to whatever practices he comes across and that dissembling is justified in the name of science. My own view is that the anthropological encounter is no more simple than any other human encounter, and is a strange mixture of the encounter of strangers and the encounters of friends (Jarvie 1968). Curiosity and self-preservation are always involved, but so are decency and respect: and respect does not endorse cheating and lying. If the anthropologist is in a position where his judgment is seriously sought by people who treat him seriously, I fail to see how he can evade his duty to be honest – unless he is in physical danger. He need not share all the views of missionaries and administrators, but he may well share some since it is their culture he comes from, and the question of what views he has and should disclose is not a simple matter. To think that natives only respect those who agree with them, or keep silent, or trickily give undirected responses,[7] may be a way of patronizing them. A fully human relationship includes disagreement and argument, anger as well as love. Barth could with instruction read Chagnon's *The Yanomamo: The Fierce People*, and *Studying the Yanomamo* for further lessons in the complexity of field relations and the unlovability of some social systems. Barth's own account in *Ritual and Knowledge Among the Baktaran of New Guinea* has a self-congratulatory and evasive air.

To sum up this discussion of methodological and practical relativism, I see it as a valuable corrective strategy, to be discarded when it undermines the moral and scientific impulses that animate the exploration of the *mores* of other peoples. Science itself is a product of our culture and social system, one most of us believe generates knowledge that is universal. But universal knowledge is not harmless, and universal knowledge and the search for it is not compatible with all social and cultural arrangements. The enterprise of science is an interventionist one *malgré lui*. It must then avoid self-deception as well as deception.

2.3 Relativism as a philosophy

This brings us to relativism at the philosophical level. Here is where I sharply take issue with Herskovits and believe anthropologists make a fundamental error in following him. Perhaps the broadest and most powerful argument I can use against relativism, one that hits both moral and cognitive, even though my concern at this point is principally with the former, is this. If relativism means something like the idea that all values are culturally induced and hence culture-bound, then anthropology in its traditional sense is impossible. For anthropology would then be simply the pretence of studying and recording 'óther' systems and their values, when in fact the anthropologist could be doing no more than projecting his own enculturated values on to what he appeared to be studying.

Let us now frame this argument in a different way. Intellectual work is the study of problems, i.e. contradictions between statements, either statements of theory contradicted by statements in fact, or statements of theory contradicted by other statements of theory. (Popper 1959; Hattiangadi 1978/9) In going to an alien society to study some problem or other the anthropologist is, then, equipped, first and foremost with some explicit and many implicit theories or theoretical ideas. These are a product of his enculturation in his 'home' culture, including his training as a social scientist. Coming to an alien culture he is on relativist assumptions simply performing an exercise in reflexivity: he is bringing his culture-bound theories to bear on his culture-bound observations and interpretations of what one might naively speak of as another society. One might well question why he bothers: it seems he cannot break out of his enculturating screen, so why not study figments of his own and other people's imagination: novels, or science fiction, for example?

This sounds far-fetched but it is a crushing point. If we are imprisoned by an enculturating screen then all we ever do is study or work out the implications of ourselves. We are engaged in navel-gazing. But then there is no reason to do anthropology, since the distinction between reality and imagination, fact and fiction, on which the possibility of science rests, does not hold. What has gone wrong here is that Herskovits's enculturation doctrine is too strong: we are enculturated, no doubt, but we are not trapped or imprisoned behind the enculturating screen. Facts, especially, are our hope for the break-through, the hope for coming into contact with the world, learning from experience.

But relativism, be it noted, is resorted to because its alternative, realism, seems mired in difficulty. How can encultured human beings work with a concept of fact and experience that transcends enculturation? That concept does not escape the screen. Positivistic views of a given real world, a world of atomic facts describable in a protocol language free of enculturation, are pipe dreams, it is true. Is such a strong absolutism the only alternative to relativism? Can there not be a weaker, critical absolutism, that treats the concept of a real world, independent of all enculturating screens, not as a secret we can penetrate once and for all, but as a regulative idea to assist our self-critical efforts to transcend the cultural screen whenever we can detect it at work? Gellner has compared this view, which is highly Kantian, to the writing of a constitution, that is, a basic set of laws by which a society agrees to be governed. He postulates as a rule of absolutist epistemology that there are no entrenched clauses. No idea, that is to say, can be held immune to challenge, including the idea that no ideas are immune to challenge. The beauty of this metaphor is how clear it makes the normative element in epistemology. Just as we say that the knowledge that all of us are biassed is no excuse for failing to try to overcome specific biasses we are aware of, so Gellner's view allows us to say that although we know we are enculturated is no excuse for failing to overcome the specific shortcomings of which we are aware.

The moral problem is a close parallel. If we are philosophical relativists then we have to picture ourselves as prisoners of the moral enculturating process that has shaped us, and if we do that, then we must accept a rather odd, and seemingly futile, picture of the act of doing fieldwork. All we could be accomplishing is to bring our enculturated moral views into contact with our enculturated moral observations: we could not even be bringing our enculturated and possibly parochial morality into contact with the real facts of the moral behaviour of other peoples. This is not logically possible on the relativist view: we are always looking through the screen. Indeed we cannot even formulate the point like that, since the idea that our morality, what we have been enculturated into, is parochial, assumes that it can be contrasted with other and less parochial moralities. This is to assume a form of detachment and transcendence that enculturating relativism declares to be impossible.

This very broad line of attack, showing the logical difficulty of extreme relativism, and showing how at the same time it makes nonsense of anthropological practice, is not going to be enough. Were it enough the preaching of relativism would long ago have stopped. This is far from being the case. Some still preach it quite overtly. Many others have retreated to surreptitious relativism, where it is hinted at, or ironical jabs are directed at those who do not display it. It is absorbed by students of anthropology who are yet totally unprepared to defend it because they have not been taught it explicitly. Indeed they are sometimes bamboozled into thinking they do not accept it, but merely practise it.

The problem for the relativist arises simply enough: Herskovits reasons that since all value judgments are enculturated, they are and can be valid only in the culture where they arise. Leaving aside the way in which this reifies an abstraction, culture, into a legitimating authority, the argument would probably be in order if all cultures came up with the same value judgments. But this is not the case. Cultures differ on both large and small matters—over suttee and the morality of eating dog meat, over infanticide and the offering of hospitality. So the question is what to make of the diversity of human moral practice, the diversity of human moral codes. Ginsberg's argument (1956) that diversity of practice conceals if not unanimity then at least convergence on a single code, we shall come to later. Perhaps the logically broadest matter over which cultures differ is their assessment of other cultures.

Most known cultures are strong absolutist. Down to very recently our culture was unreservedly absolutist. Relativist sentiments are very ancient but they usually emerge within an absolutist culture. How can an enculturating screen teach some of us to see it as nothing other than that: a local peculiarity? And does not the vision of us as all screened already transcend screening?

Certainly the argument that those customs which differ from what the speaker's society accepts are morally objectionable is not a valid argument. But the opposite position, that because customs differ they are all morally equal and to be given blanket endorsement is not valid either. Difference is neither good in itself nor bad in itself. This is easily shown. Some cultures are racialist and practise discrimination against minorities, strangers, foreigners, outsiders or those of other religious persuasions. If the anthropologist winks at this he himself becomes a racialist at one remove. In other words, does the cultural relativist mean to condone or even endorse racialism, child-murder, discrimination, prejudice, and so on? There is no doubt that this is a very tricky question on the practical as well as the theoretical level.

For the relativist anthropologist has used a mixture of empirical and philosophical reasoning to paint himself into a practical corner. His humanitarian impulse to respect and tolerate others may now conflict with his equally humanitarian impulse to help and teach them. Moreover, he refuses to extend his respect and toleration to those of his countrymen who suppress suttee, infanticide and dog meat, as well as go out to preach the gospel of our lord in the colonies. The cultural relativist can argue that he withholds respect because these activities of suppression, while morally approved in the culture of the suppressors, cross the boundary of enculturation and thus become *ultra vires*. This reply ignores what I have already pointed out, that many if not most cultures extend the writ of their moral judgments beyond their cultural boundaries. On what ground can the anthropologist select out those boundary-crossing judgments and say they are not to be tolerated or endorsed? As parts of living cultures they are unassailable.

In the last analysis the problem of relativism is what philosophers call reflexive; it is not so much about moral judgments, as about moral judgments about moral judgments or systems of moral judgment. Moral judgments are self-regarding. We sometimes judge other moral views to be themselves immoral. This reflexivity is difficult to escape. Faced with diverse moral views we can either say there is no way to judge between them, so they are all equally moral or immoral; or we can say, moral judgments are confined to the cultural and social systems in which they emerged, and, since there can be no valid intersystemic judgments as they would not stem from a cultural or social system, then there is no means of comparing and assessing them. So, either all moralities are equal, or, moralities are non-comparable and the question of equality doesn't arise. But both of these judgments are themselves extra-systemic and hence suspect on the relativists' own premisses.

Put simply, from what social and political context does the moral judgment that diverse moral systems are equal draw its validity? The answer is, of course, it draws it from the context of western society and culture that has given birth both to liberal tolerance and to anthropology. Western thought is imperialistic, tries to conquer other thought systems; western morality is also imperialistic in that it too tries to conquer other moralities. Most other cultures in contact situations are the same, especially when they are literate or when their system has cognitive power. The difference is that in the west there is also this self-conscious stuff about objective, scientific, tolerant and respectful scientific inquiry.

2.4 The case for and against relativism

Summing up so far, when we strip away all the sophisticated manoeuvres I think the case for relativism reduces to two arguments. One of these arguments is invalid, the other is entirely negative. The negative I have already objected to, the invalid argument is one to be sympathized with. The invalid argument stems from the noble aspiration to respect rather than denigrate the views of other people. The negative argument holds that there is no way to solve the reflexivity problem – to sustain the claim that there are trans-cultural or cross-cultural values; that they can be justified.

The invalid argument goes like this: premiss, *let us respect not denigrate the moral views of other people*. Premiss, *such views are a result of enculturation*. Premiss, *enculturation takes place within cultures*. Conclusion, *let us therefore relativize views to cultures*, universally phrased prescriptions or proscriptions (e.g. 'Honour thy Father and thy Mother', or 'cruelty is wrong') should be interpreted as having the suppressed qualifier, 'this is moral in this culture'. The argument is so invalid it is hard to formulate. Respect for the views of others can be expressed by many other means than relativism and relativism may contain elements of condescension – the opposite of respect. Trouble begins with the first premiss. The peoples we are busy respecting may themselves not respect that premiss. Our relativistic modesty is not widely shared. This leads to the further point that the premiss is a moral view and to be consistent must be relativized to our culture – it has no universal validity. Yet we know it is contentious since our anthropological ancestors displayed ethnocentric attitudes. If we are sensitive we know full well that many people in our culture do not respect other cultures, so our culture enculturates people into both the premiss of respect and that of lack of respect. Why, then, should anthropology be premissed on only one of the two possible views promoted by our culture?

The answer to this question goes to the second argument – on what basis can we erect a trans-cultural morality? The same basis we use to choose between competing moralities in our culture? And what basis is that? It is a basis without a base. Bases, like revealed religion, do not solve the problem because some people do not accept them and others can simply question in a Kantian manner where *they* get *their* authority.

How do we decide moral issues? We argue them out. We especially concentrate on three lines of attack that are being exemplified in this work: factual inadequacy, inconsistency, and consequences. Arguing against relativism I have tried to show that we cannot in fact live by it, and, since ought implies can, cannot implies not-ought; I have endeavoured to show it to be inconsistent; and I shall now try to show it has unacceptable consequences, i.e. consequences inconsistent with other moral views we hold, tacitly and explicitly.

1 Relativism ends up by saying what is, is right: that a culture is the way it is and, that its morality endorses that way, implies, on relativist premisses, that what is is right. But what if both the way things are seems immoral and the endorsing of the way things are as moral seems immoral also? Are these thoughts one is somehow not allowed to articulate? Do they reveal some depths of superiorist thinking?

2 This posture of what is is right is itself conservative and antiliberal, since it denounces in advance the forces of change and toleration if they come from outside – whatever 'inside' and 'outside' mean here. But societies, even entrenchedly conservative ones, change, sometimes with startling abruptness, as in Iran in 1979. Up to the last moment established morality has been endorsing the status quo and denouncing change. Yet once the change comes about *it* now has to be endorsed. This is the classic Hobbesian problem that the only revolutions that are justified are those that have already taken place.

3 Cultures or societies are neither homogeneous nor seamless: hence to be tolerant and accepting of them and their morality is vague advice. What exactly is one to be tolerant and accepting

of? There may be both an establishment and a protest movement, and many shades in between. To what is a member of this society enculturated, then? What if he is enculturated to believe the official teachings and preachings are all lies and hypocrisy and only outsiders like tourists and anthropologists can be turned to for enlightenment? (This is not so far-fetched; there is a lot of this in the Communist block countries.) What if the signals are confused and both the doctrines of respect for and condescension towards other moralities is preached?

4   Relativism all-too-easily reduces to nihilism. In a way what we call a culture is not 'there' – I have called it an abstraction: it is something we construct, build or imagine to make things coherent. Once one sees this one also sees that although our constructs may be co-ordinated (as I have explained in *Concepts and Society*), they need not be. If they are not, then each of us mentally constructs something different as culture and hence each of us endorses acculturation to something different. In fact each of us becomes his own judge of morality (and reality), which is a poor premiss for a scientist to begin with. Moreover, for each of us to say what is right is a formula for moral chaos and nihilism.

5   A final consequence of relativism is this — it reduces the notion of respect for others to 'agrees with' or 'endorses'. Yet in our own culture the most famous expression of respect is the slogan, 'I completely disagree with your views but I will die for your right to express them!' Respect has little or nothing to do with agreement. Perhaps we need to learn how to respect diversity and yet disagree with it. When it comes to head-hunting and eating dogs British colonizers found this beyond their capacity. But in the regulation of land tenure, marriage, inheritance and such like they often enshrined local custom in law. The lesson here is that neither respect nor understanding implies agreement.

Let me go back over these numbered points to see if they can be dealt with frontally.

1'   It is not the case that might is right. On the contrary, might is, very characteristically, wrong. Only in a caricature of a tradition-bound society is might declared to be right. The relativist exaggerates the homogeneity and seamlessness of cultures and moralities. Nearly all moral systems, i.e. those subsystems of cultures we call their moral systems, nearly all of them are in a constant state of flux, dispute, argument and review. Otherwise why would most societies have mediators and judges? But if what we so glibly call a moral system is more a social system than some articulable set of beliefs and principles what does this do to the relativist's omni-tolerance? It impales him, among other things, on contradictions; because in endorsing local morality he may be endorsing simultaneously contradictory views. More important, it gives the anthropologist some moral space of his own. While being reticent and respectful he nevertheless has an obligation to his own views on the matters at hand and, if asked to articulate them would be derelict in his duty to his own moral system (both the general one and the specialized one of scholars and scientists) were he to dissemble, pretend he had no views, or otherwise evade. Respect for others presumably means something like not condescending to them, not shielding them for their own good (in fact for your own good, i.e. as salve to a guilty conscience). The fact is that if the anthropologist has been properly enculturated in western society (a moot point, since so many of them are socially marginal) then he will go to any lengths to avoid infanticide. Confronted with infanticide on the streets of New York or Los Angeles he would be a coward if he did nothing. What is different if he is confronted with infanticide in Africa? The child and its call on him as a moral being are the same, for we assume in both cases he has no connection with it. Practical arguments from personal danger aside, what is the morality of the matter? At the very least a forceful expression of his views and an offer to explain them?

2′   Change is a topic anthropologists have always been ambivalent about. One of their long-term projects has been to record the main features of all extant societies before they are altered or dispersed. This streak of antiquarianism sometimes shows itself in stronger form when they ally themselves with forces resisting change. Such change stems predominantly from the economic and political forces generalized as 'modernization'. Wage-labour itself can totally disrupt a society based, let us say, on kinship obligation. If a tribe is forced to wear clothes it has to start operating in such a way that money can be made to purchase the clothing. On the whole anthropologists have argued that remote societies have a way of life they are entitled to and which is worth preserving. Some have collaborated with governments the better to cushion the worst impact of imposed changes on the people they study. Others have become militant advocates of resistance to change. In Canada, Inuit and other native peoples have vigorously opposed development of the Arctic. Many of the arguments smack of those generated by anthropologists. Yet it is not clear change might not bring benefit.

3′   This applies to the divisions within society too. There are at least two sides to every question, and often more. Relativism is a hopeless platform for responsible decision-making. That can only come from making up one's own mind by the use of reason, weighing and assessing arguments and premisses, for their consistency, consequences and factual adequacy.

4' I have no doubt that the relativist has an answer to these urgings. Perhaps it could go like this. When we talk for example of believing in the rule of law, we don't mean rule of a law (namely ours), we mean some system of law which may differ from place to place, and indeed is expected to do so. So with morality, we do not want to endorse chaos or lack of morality but some local moral system.

What in turn I should say to this is that only Hobbes believed *any* system of law was better than none; most of us would say that when we say we believe in the rule of law we mean in a rule of law that is just – and this is a transcultural judgment. We may wonder where it comes from, and in the third part of this monograph I shall endeavour to show that it comes from our rationality. At all events, it is preferable to Herskovits's considered view:

> There is, indeed, some reason to feel that the concept of freedom should be realistically redefined as the right to be exploited in terms of the patterns of one's own culture. (1973, p. 9)

5' Respect should not include respect for exploitation, immorality, lies, superstition, and so on. Just because these are the categories of that western culture that gave birth to science and social science does not make them culturally relative. Our culture, like most cultures, formulates its value judgments in universal and categorical form. This is not a philosophical mistake. We *mean* to reach beyond the immediate, we mean to articulate in the name of the whole of mankind. The universally available tools of reason being applied to the tasks of assessment is the most serious form our human responsibility to ourselves and others can take.

By an historical or sociological account of the origins of relativism we can come to understand anthropologists as in reaction against the crimes and misdeeds (non-relative judgments!) of their forebears who came into contact with primitive peoples. Such are the depredations wrought by European colonists and missionaries upon the peoples of the world that no one any longer wants to be associated with them. On the contrary, our impulse is to incorporate those far-away peoples into our moral community and accord them the dignity and respect we accord our own members. This is a noble ideal with which I fully sympathize. It has not, however, become embodied in relativism. I think I have shown how the relativist in fact involves himself in a condescending, not an egalitarian, stance towards primitive peoples; and I have also shown how the primitive peoples themselves and their often

85

rebarbative moralities cannot be conveniently ignored. It takes two to make a moral community. In the absence of such two-way co-operation the problem becomes much more subtle and interesting, and relativism just a gross and uninteresting policy.

2.5 Relativism and diversity

I turn back now to the argument from the diversity of morals which is the historical origin of relativism.

A The first and most powerful argument on the road to relativism seems to be the fact of diversity in human custom. To be more precise, the same action may be considered moral in one society and immoral in another. If one assumes the premiss that societies cannot be ranked in a way that makes the judgment of one override the judgment of another in these matters, then this means the question of whether such and such an action is or is not immoral cannot be answered. Instead the question has to be rephrased as, 'moral or immoral from the point of view of this society'. This moves us towards relativism one step.
Herskovits sums it up thus:

> Cultural relativism developed because the facts of differences in these concepts of reality or in moral systems . . . forced the realization of the problem of finding valid cross-cultural norms. In every case where criteria to evaluate the ways of different peoples have been proposed . . . the question has at once posed itself: 'Whose standards?' (1958, p. 270)

B Not only is there disagreement about how to slot actions into the moral categories, there is also a lack of agreement between different societies as to what the moral categories are. For example some societies may not have the category 'cruelty'; others may rank the categories differently; still others may have categories like 'face' or 'honour' that scarcely exist any more in our society.[8] Again, assuming that people and societies are in some sense equal, it follows that there are no fixed categories of morality, and how an act should be classified can be discussed only relative to social (or cultural) units.

C So, while all societies have morality, their particular moralities differ as well as overlap, and there appears to be no way of transcending society to evaluate these clashes (from which society would these standards come?). It seems to follow that there are no universal moral rules, there are no absolute values.

The consequence of all this is that all moralities are equal. If society X differs from society Y over a moral matter then both are right. What is, is right. What is, it so happens, is decided by power and force – what else? Moreover, whatever is enforced as right, is right and must be obeyed – on what grounds can it be dissented from? An alternative view has as it were no claim, since it is not enforced and hence is not the morality of that society. On the contrary, by appealing to any other legitimation, whether local or transcendental, it de-legitimates itself.

The logic of this argument is not usually pushed through, but I think it should be. Not only is it true that societies differ on moral matters: but individuals within societies differ on moral matters too. Think of divisions between Protestants about war, the death penalty, abortion, permissiveness, punishment. And this despite the fact that they may well appeal ostensibly to the same moral system to buttress their claims. But if a system of moral authority is susceptible of different interpretations then the question arises of which interpretation is correct. For example, there are Christians who maintain that only pacifism is compatible with their religion, and there are Christians who can reconcile their religion to patriotic wars and there are Christians who supported the Crusades. In Iran there are zealots intent on killing people for all sorts of crimes in the name of Islam, and there are others who say all this is against the spirit of the religion. Cargo-cult societies embody such variation of moral opinion openly.

So, even if moral systems are legitimated by social embedding, and even if there are not alternative systems competing within the society, the given system still has to be interpreted. If the clashes of interpretation are between groups then presumably again morality is settled by a struggle for power. If it is not then we must raise doubts as to whether the society in question has anything corresponding to a single, coherent system of morality. If the clashes of interpretation are between individuals, if, as a thought experiment, we imagine that every man has his own interpretation, then it looks as though we have no morality at all, because moral systems are socially or culturally limited, they cannot be validated relative to single individuals.

Later, in the next part of this monograph, I shall show how these arguments can be generalized to the cognitive field and yield an epistemological relativism. I do not treat it in detail here because there is a seriousness to moral relativism that is lacking in epistemological relativism. Moral relativism has perhaps poor arguments in its favour but the highest and most admirable of motives. Epistemological relativism is, I am sorry to say, more like a plaything for intellectuals, a doctrine that no one takes seriously for a minute, but which is preached mainly because people argue themselves into it and then can't find any way out. Such a presumption on common sense is frivolous.

Peter Winch, who does not refer to Herskovits and who, I think, does not like to be called a relativist, has developed the enculturation of values argument most carefully by fusing the data of Evans-Pritchard with the philosophy of the later Wittgenstein (1958, 1964). His manoeuvre goes something like this. The meaning of what we say and do can be found by attending to the use we make of what we say and do. Use involves seeking out the patterns or rules to which our saying and doing seem to conform. Rules and patterns looked at generally seem to go to make up what we might call forms of life: forms are clusters of coherent and connected rules. These forms of life are the reference point for meaning. 'Forms of life', an expression that comes from Wittgenstein, is not the same as culture or society (indeed it is not quite clear what it is as a glance at the exegetes will show[9]), but it is not wholly unlike that either. In Winch's use, forms of life seem to be intra-cultural as well as inter-cultural: he treats religion and science as forms of life, as well as Britain and the Azande. But for a moment stick to the *inter*. For Winch, truth, rationality and logic itself are bound to forms of life.[10] If the Azande are uninterested in consistency that shows that what they will accept as logic is perhaps different from what we will. Of course, by this logic, the problem of relativism can easily be resolved. If we are as it were free to choose our own logic then those of us who oppose relativism can simply attach ourselves to conventional logic and demand consistency and apply that standard wherever we see fit: culturally and interculturally. Moreover, where there is an inconsistency we can simply insist that it has to be smoothed out.

Even more simply, we can dismiss the arguments of the anti-relativists by showing that from a contradiction everything follows so there will be no refuting, hence no arguing with, those who repudiate logic. Then why bother?

Faced with some of these bewildering and even nihilistic consequences of relativism there are those anthropologists and others who back away from it and seek an exit. I want to discuss three of these exits and show that however plausible they may appear, they are nevertheless rather weak and don't do the trick.

*Exit*₁. The Ginsberg manoeuvre goes something like this.[11] True there are diverse moral views and practices around the world, but there is also an interesting amount of overlap and agreement. Murder, theft and adultery, for example, are penalized everywhere; courage and honesty valued. Perhaps we can overcome the diversity of morals by attending to this overlap and agreement. Indeed, on an evolutionary scale, as it were, the fact of agreement might represent some sort of convergence, a core of moral ideas on which there is agreement surrounded by an accretion of lesser ideas. Areas of disagreement are those which are less important, less central, and on which agreement is less urgently required. The rational man seeking moral guidance in the chaos of diversity might look to these cores of agreement and use them as a starting point, at least, to work his way out of the chaotic diversity.

There are two troubles with the Ginsberg manoeuvre. The first is that consensus does not legitimate ideas because we can always make the judgment that the consensus view is morally mistaken, and we can even judge the consensus *method* of deciding any moral issue to be itself morally mistaken. If we are told that 85 percent of the peoples of the world live in societies that do not condone but strongly penalize murder, we are still at liberty to argue that they are mistaken and the other 15 percent are right, and, further, to maintain that it is immoral to try to decide moral issues by statistics.

The second trouble is that the areas of disagreement, diversity, are being wished away rather than reasoned away. It has to be shown that areas of disagreement are less rather than more important, and that we might better concentrate on them. In science, after all, the problematic areas where we expect change and growth are precisely those where scientists disagree. Lack of moral convergence and consensus might similarly be areas of moral growth and progress. Popkin has argued that the radical millenarianism of the seventeenth century paved the way for the rational and secular enlightenment of the eighteenth. The same might be true of cargo cults. Radical dissent from the colonial morality can be a learning experience not only for the cargo cultists but also for the colonial administrators and missionaries. Values of orderly administration and of Christian worship might, after dialogue with cultists, come to seem low on any reasonable priority scale. Thus diversity-relativism is incoherent.

Exit₂, the G. E. Moore manoeuvre,[12] proceeds somewhat differently by arguing that the source of morality is not some system of codes or rules, those rather are the effects of what might be called a basic moral intuition with which we are all endowed. We may learn and refine this in our upbringing, but it legitimates morality, not the other way around. Hence, the diversity of morals is to be handled by referring back to our basic moral intuitions (knowledge of the good) and acting in accordance with them, regardless of the prevailing view here or elsewhere. Apart from the trouble you can get in if your intuitions are grossly discrepant from those of others in your surroundings, there is the little matter of disputes being unresolvable: you appeal to your intuitions, I appeal to mine and we may end up with moral chaos again. So much for intuitionist relativism.

Exit₃, the evolutionist manoeuvre, is to look at the diversity of morals and ask whether there is change, and to ask whether the change has any direction. That is to say, can we see evidence in our society or in the scene as a whole of something like moral progress? Can we see codes developing greater universality: treating all men and eventually all men and women alike? Can we see codes being more just? Can we see greater humanity and compassion displayed towards wrongdoers in their treatment and punishment? Duncker (1939) offers a variant of this when he maintains that valuation turns on meaning and meaning is a function of its social situation. For example, infanticide may be not murder but a sacrifice to the gods, or a guaranteed entry into heaven for the child. Hence he concludes: 'given the same situational meanings an act is likely to receive the same ethical valuation. If an act is found to receive different valuations at different times or places, this is generally found to be due to different meanings' (p. 44). In fact, 'the same act, being the same with regard to all meanings involved, has never been observed to incur different valuations' (p. 50). Bravery, justice, generosity have never been seen as vices. This does not mean relativism or lack of moral evolution. 'One step in the history of mankind which can lay claim to the title of moral evolution or progress . . . the advance from a conception of man as an incarnation of magical forces to the conception of man as a self-centred ("Moral") personality' (p. 52).

In more modern terms we might say that any act can be included under numerous different descriptions. If we are to debate relativism we have, of course to ensure that we are talking about the same act, with the same meaning, i.e. under the same description. The problems with this exit are fairly blatant. The notion of progress is itself a moral one and so can hardly be introduced *ex nihilo* in order to assess the shortcomings and triumphs of moral systems. So we can't defend evolutionary relativism.

Where does all this leave us, then? At an impasse? The complete picture of the way out I propose comes in part three because it is intimately connected with the view of human rationality I am also engaged in putting forward. A preliminary sketch is required at this stage if the reader is not to be left hanging by the basically destructive series of arguments I have been busy marshalling *in re* relativism. To begin with, relativism's first mistake is to argue that we can evade the responsibility of making assessments and judgments by relating them to culture: there is no way this can be avoided. Even to declare them relative to culture is itself an evaluation stemming from this culture and hence denying the universalist and transcendental claims of many of the systems being discussed. The believer in Islam, like the Roman Catholic, most definitely does not consider his morality culture bound: it is universally applicable and absolutely true. Whether he or she chooses militantly to implement this view is a matter of individual choice that does not affect the logic of his position. So cultural relativism, posing as neutral arbiter between views, clashes with those which do not allow there to be a neutral arbiter.

Relativism also clashes with practice: few are the anthropologists who do not have strong moral views about some of the stuff they observe. Turnbull and Chagnon simply wrote it down. In practice one has views, and to reassure oneself that they are merely a matter of enculturation is no comfort. We might be torn by the conviction that were the societies we are studying to gain a little in affluence it might be possible for them also to develop different and perhaps more humane means of ordering their social intercourse.

To go further: it is immoral and irresponsible to preach and attempt to practise relativism. It is on a par with walking by on the other side of the street when you see a person being attacked. Hatch (1983, p. 95) utilizes the self-same image: if we hear screams coming from a dark alley how can we walk away and maintain it is none of our business? It is of course possible that we got it wrong, that the screams are theatre, or are of pleasure, or the apparent villain is victim, but these hypotheticals do not excuse indifference. Neither the decision to help nor its implementation involves any assumption of our superiority to those involved, merely urgent moral concern. It does, however, involve one distinction Hatch overlooks: that between the actor and the intervener, between the self and the other, between the observer and the observed. Our conception of ourselves as acting agents involves the idea of separateness, of boundaries between them and us. The test of the existence of such boundaries consists in our view that the screams are not there merely because we are, are not therefore figments of our imaginations, they would be there even if we were not, would continue were we to pass by. So we have the option of moving the boundary of ourselves towards the boundary of the person screaming to engage in interaction.

No doubt this comparison will seem shocking and unfair. I don't think it is, and I think anthropologists who preach relativism preach it innocently with the excellent motives and bad logic I have outlined. We have a responsibility to science and we have a responsibility as human beings. Every human being has a call on

91

us, and, no matter what the excuse, if we spurn that call, we are not acting responsibly or morally, and we are undervaluing the peoples with whom we are in contact. What we owe our fellow man, as scientists and as members of the moral community, is respect. If he does not respect us as a matter of principle (because we are white, Jewish or whatever) it is absurd to adopt a stance of relativist indifference. The respect we owe him (leaving aside that we owe it to ourselves to protect our own safety first) entails that we not blind ourselves to his prejudices, but inform him of them, and try our best to indicate that the good life can be lived without the benefit of these props, or, if it cannot, that it is better to impoverish life a little than to endorse such mistakes. Notice that I am concentrating on the acute situation where the visitor is himself the victim of his own relativism. I stress again and again that we must not infantilize those we are in contact with. Our moral views are not some enculturated accident, nor some automatically adjusted evolutionary strategy. They are (or should be) carefully thought-out attempts to regulate the relations of human beings both as to means and as to ends. Those with whom we disagree may have different values, in which case we have a clash to negotiate, or they may not have thought things out clearly or thoroughly enough. Either way we learn from them and about them by disclosing ourselves and our thinking and judgment. Anything less is indefensible.

Part three

Rationality and relativism

In my discussion of rationality I argued a series of points: (1) that we should generalize the sociological model of rational action as goal-directed action, and subsume under it so-called rational thinking, rather than vice versa; (2) that rational thinking is a problem-solving activity and the paradigm of problem-solving is science (not chess); hence (3) the usual elevation of science into a model of rationality would make sense. It is not hard to see how these points, if accepted, would pose an awkward dilemma for anthropologists. Most of the societies they study do not have science. A principal goal of anthropology is to give a rational reconstruction of such pre-scientific societies and their customs as being goal-directed and hence intelligible. Yet when anthropologists come to the cognitive systems of these societies, to their practical and theoretical knowledge-claims, to their world-views and cosmologies, they cannot gainsay the fact that these fall somewhat short of science.

Various strategies for evading the obvious conclusion—that there is a limit to the rationality of the societies anthropologists study—were discussed in § 1.6. If rationality has to do with goal-directedness, and if the most effective efforts to achieve goals are those based on correct information about the world, then the possibility (not the fact) of rationality increases linearly with the growth of knowledge. Thus, while it does not follow that societies possessing science are more rational than those without, it does follow that such societies have the greater potential rationality and the potential to improve their own degree of rationality.

This grates on anthropologists' sensibilities because it smacks of late nineteenth-century evolutionist anthropology with its assumption of the all-round superiority of European society.[1] If, however, the rationality of science consists not so much of thought processes of a special and exclusive kind, but of a means of organizing thought, of a set of social institutions, then we need deny no society some rationality and potential for more. To say that this society invented the transistor but that this one did not is no slur; and it need be no slur to say that this society invented the social institutions of science and that this did not. Both transistors and science are exportable, although success with the latter is harder to achieve.

In the second part of this monograph, I argued that moral relativism is untenable for the simple reaon that it is condescending, it does not take moral disagreement seriously. It gives blanket endorsement to alternative systems, leaving one's own system unchallenged and intact. This is to entrench, to circumscribe, alternatives; the only function such circumscription can have is to protect oneself. Only a genuinely reflective dialogue embodies the ideals of rationality (applying reason to the task of learning from experience) and respect.

Rationality and relativism, I suggested, were two of the fundamental problems of anthropology: the problem of making sense of societies and the problem of comparing societies. The third problem to which I come now, was that of the relation of rationality to relativism, the problem of reconciling the rational unity of mankind with the moral unity of mankind.

The problem of the relation of rationality and relativism has two parts: is it rational to be a moral absolutist rather than a moral relativist; and is it moral to be a rationalist? These formulations are somewhat gnomic, so I will unpack them before proceeding. At the beginning of this monograph we formulated the problem of the rational unity of mankind as what demarcates man from the beasts. The solution was that mankind is united in possessing the disposition and capacity to apply reason to tasks in order continually to get better at applying reason to tasks. The problem of relativism is that of sustaining the idea that mankind is a moral unity as well as a rational one in the face of the diversity of human moral systems in actual practice.

What is the relation of this idea of moral unity to that of rational unity? Are they simply two possible uniting ideas plucked out of all the logical possibilities? My contention shall be that they are opposite faces of each other. That my model of the rational unity of mankind envisages mankind as a moral community; that my vision of the moral community reasoning together is also a rational unity.

One task to which we apply reason is that of life together. Human beings necessarily live in groups because of the demands of sexual reproduction and because many earthly environments are too hostile for the single individual to survive in them. The result of reflection on this problem is what we call morality: rules to live by.

The disposition and capacity to apply reason to tasks is what we use to cope with our environment. The better to survive together we utilize reason.

We see then that applying reason to living together yields morality, and applying morality to living together yields reason. There is thus a link between rationality and relativism: the problems are formulated together and solved together. A rationality which also allows relativism is self-defeating; relativism cannot be sustained in the face of rationality.

I shall proceed to deal with these topics in four sections: 3.1 Relativism in its cognitive dimension; 3.2 The connection of rationality with weak absolutism; 3.3 The connection of weak absolutism with rationality. A fourth section can also stand as an epilogue: Anthropology as sociocultural transcendence.

3.1 Relativism in its cognitive dimension

The connection of morality and learning may be hard to grasp, so I shall proceed now to show how moral relativism generalizes into cognitive relativism and how that in turn undermines rationality. We can then consider the connection of moral to cognitive relativism and set up the discussion of the rationality-relativism issue.

The relativism that is particularly influential these days is general cognitive relativism, a quite extraordinary generalization of moral relativism. Corresponding to the diversity of morals, there is the diversity of cognition. We in the West have some very clear ideas about where jeeps and lanterns and tinned food come from. Melanesian cargo cultists have very different ideas. Any naive suggestion that we are correct and they are mistaken can be dispelled by experiment. Yali, a cargo cult leader, had spent time in Australia and was by no means unaware that consumer goods were produced by work and organization. But it was after he returned that he was gradually sucked into the cargo cults of his culture. Of course, one could simply conjure up a 'primitive mentality' incapable of grasping the truth about things, but that is hardly compatible with the rational unity of mankind.

Yali . . . assumed that white men had God and Jesus Christ, who were ultimately responsible for their material culture. This did not conflict with what he saw or otherwise learnt of industrial Australia: the sugar mill, brewery, tinned meat and fish factories, and the aircraft repair shop. He was aware that Europeans could make their own goods, but he nevertheless believed that their God had taught them the requisite secular techniques . . . Moreover, the Europeans' God could, if properly invoked, supplement human production by sending cargo ready made and direct in times of shortage and adversity. This explained the vast fleets of ships and aircraft which suddenly came to New Guinea during the war (Lawrence 1964, p. 128).

Such a case is a great tonic to the relativist. He thinks it shows that reality (and hence the truth of where jeeps come from) is a social construction that varies from society to society across the earth. For Yali cargo *is* the explanation of what happens. The struggle for what you believe in must go on.

Westerners must try to accept Cargo on its own terms, not theirs, for Cargo is a reality, even though their western-conditioned minds tell them it is impossible. . . . For, in a sense any expectation of a reward or a return, gratuitously given by some other 'force', physical or intangible, might be described as Cargo (Rice 1974, p. xv).

From the sharp clash of views about how things are and from the seeming irresolubility of disputes about them it is easy to infer that there must be some large or more general barrier to communication. The culprits can be identified as truth and logic. We westerners operate under the view that what is true, is true once and for all, here, now and everywhere for all time. Similarly, we operate with a notion of logic, of principles of inference, that are universally valid in all languages and cultures. But what if we want to say that Yali is correct in his culture and we are correct in our culture? What if we want to say that the logic that we think of as inexorable, e.g. a jeep is either made by machines or it is not, is challenged by a logic that says that jeeps are made by machines *and* they are not because they are made by the spirits? Certainly there is no way this dispute can be resolved. As a model for such a dispute we can take Lewis Carroll's famous paper on how to convince a doubting Thomas: in this case a doubting tortoise.[2] If someone does not accept an inference that seems to you transparent, no amount of additional premisses attempting to make the transparency transparent will serve to shift the doubter. As Bartley (1962) shows in his classic discussion of this paper, the argument has turned from one about the world to one about logic, it has moved to the meta-level and is not straightforward at all. When logic is in dispute logic will not help, but meta-logic might.

The relativist doesn't know about meta-logic, he knows only that there is a dispute that seems irresoluble.

It seems that when a dispute is irresoluble then the choice of sides, the backing of the winner, can no longer be decided by truth or by logic. Truth and logic can be invoked only after sides have been taken; truth and logic are tied to, or are relative to, the system of ideas one chooses to attach oneself to. The most general systems of ideas are called cultures.[3] So it might seem that truth and logic are relative to cultures. In a plural culture like our own this picture is slightly complicated because the language bounds a culture-area in which there are many subcultures that have their own ideas about logic and truth: the various systems of religion, including secular religions like Marxism and Freudianism, their irrationalist, dogmatic and traditionalist proponents all seeming to fly in face of any general logic and any standard notion of truth. Truth and logic are functions of the ultimate commitments embedded in general belief systems. Such ultimate commitments need not be thought of as conscious choices in the face of dilemmas.[4] On the cultural scene they are far more likely to be positions to which people have been enculturated long before they were aware there were choices to make. Communication, on this commitment view, basically only takes place within cultures sharing ultimate commitments and hence notions of truth and logic. Cross-cultural communication, in the sense of dispute about what is so and what is not cannot take place. Shifts of position by cultures, or subcultures, whether over time or not have to be explained sociologically, by 'impact' phenomena such as drift, depredations of oral tradition, inanition, intrusion, syncretism, schism, political revolution.

Commitment denies the idea that rationality is a bootstrap process of constant attempts to improve our achievement by given standards and of attempts to improve those standards themselves (see Agassi 1973 and Briskman 1977).

That logic and truth and hence rationality are culture-specific is a radical relativism and, I am inclined to think, clashes with the facts. Such evidence as I have seen suggests that most primitive peoples understand intuitively the principles of good argument; have a correspondence theory of truth; and distinguish rational conduct much as we do. Yet a whole school of thought exists that denies this. There is Peter Winch, D. Z. Phillips, Rush Rhees and, in some incarnations, A. MacIntyre. Their views are congruent with those of Toulmin who (1958) argued that logic is not even universal to our own culture – it is not uniformly used. We are being rational when we act as lawyers, or inductive scientists, so that category of the rational has to be seen as broader than that of logic.[5] Formulated thus, it would not clash with my own position. Certainly rationality – goal-directed action – is a broader category than action that conforms to the rules of logic. The issue comes over just how the broader and narrower are thought to relate to each other. The post-Wittgensteinian writers I have referred to think the broader can only be captured by some extra-logical explication. Whereas my suggestion is to see logic as the structure or skeleton of rationality and to formulate the programme not of going beyond logic (and abandoning, for example, the rules of valid inference as Toulmin does), but, rather, of expanding and enriching logic. My model here, clearly, is Popper's path-breaking work in *The Logic of Scientific Discovery* where, while strictly conforming to the basic rules of logic, he offered other rules for the rational conduct of science to supplement them.

What makes the Wittgensteinians take up their posture? Apologetics for their secret or not so secret religious convictions which they want to shield from the harsh criticism of logic and the facts? The desire to have a philosophy that leaves everything as it is, which reifies basic British bourgeois complacency (Gellner 1959)? In this they have different motives from the other great relativist input: Mannheim's sociology of knowledge that is an outgrowth of the Marxist notion of 'false consciousness' and the reality principle, but which draws back from unchecked cultural relativism.

What can be said against cultural relativism? Does none of our learning, does not especially the cognitive power of science, transcend it? Can we not discriminate good from bad goals, stultifying from liberating institutions, efficient from inefficient customs?

Four ways of making such discriminations and hence of escaping the consequences of cultural relativism are known to me, that of the *sociology of knowledge*, that of *pragmatism*, that of *Winch* and that of the view which I espouse. Each of these is different.

Escape 1: sociology of knowledge. Mathematics and logic were sacred for Mannheim, as was, in his later work, science. This creates the dilemma, what about the science of sociology? Mannheim was a committed sociologist, so he opted for considering sociology a transcending science, and hence its practitioners in some way enlightened, freed from the conditioning of the total ideology in which they were otherwise enculturated, able to see beyond the screen. The trouble is, to everyone else this looks like wishful thinking.[6] If the sociologist can exempt himself from socioanalysis, can see through his own enculturating screen, then maybe others can too. Mannheim's arguments, like Herskovits's, were too strong: they sprang the self-referring trap.

Escape 2: pragmatism. Pragmatism is the (relativist) view that what is true is what works, and that what works may from time to time and place to place be very different. Hence 'true' is relative to time and/or place, what Duncker (1939) calls 'situation'. So it is not that relativism leads nowhere, but rather that it confines us to *in situ* appraisal of goals, customs and institutions. If they work, well and good, if not they are wanting. The simplest objection to pragmatism is that we have reasons to think that some things that work are untrue, and what is true sometimes will not work. Connecting the two makes it difficult to explain changes and fixities in our ideas, which we usually attribute to the effort to bring the two into line.

Escape 3: Winch Has been patented by Peter Winch – each society has its own concepts, its own 'world', and yet they connect with each other somehow through their common confrontation with the basic facts of human life: not earth, air and fire, but birth, copulation and death – these are conceptualized by all cultures and hence we have some sort of benchmark for beginning cross-cultural dialogue. This solution is very Ginsberg-ish.[7]

Communication, however, implies disagreement as well as agreement; stressing the one at the expense of the other is inadequate. Winch wants to explore and wonder at other systems of conceptualizing birth, copulation and death. Magic is the web of thought that cannot think itself to be wrong. This, as other negative commentators were quick to point out, endorses Christianity as well as Azande witchcraft.

As I have endeavoured to explain elsewhere (1970), the key problem is that Winch shifts the task of anthropology from that of explaining other cultures to that of understanding other cultures. The two are very different: there are clear criteria for explanation, none for understanding. Practitioners of a local culture can be said to understand it. They can also, without inconsistency, be said to be utterly unable to explain it. The situation might be compared to the buyers and sellers at a street market. All they may know is that they assemble regularly and engage in trade. If we want an explanation of why they do so, and why in certain ways, and why there are certain outcomes, economics, not the informants, is where we should seek help.

Similarly with belief systems. They may be understood by their believers in a limited sense, or in a sense that sets the standard, but they cannot explain themselves. Furthermore, in fact, belief systems are constructs – abstractions from the congeries of beliefs, doubts, qualifications, idiosyncratic twists that make up the ideas on the ground. People do not necessarily know of themselves as part of a belief-system, just as the idea that people always know

101

what to do and what they are doing in social life is naive. They are often doubtful and uncertain. This applies to conduct, values and beliefs.

3.2 The connection of weak absolutism with rationality

Escape 4: comes from the work of Popper, Agassi, Bartley and Gellner. We do as a matter of course make cross-cultural and interpersonal value judgments without any sense of inappropriateness. We do make transcultural, transpersonal knowledge claims (magic is false, e.g.) without guilt. Most important: communication precedes language (else how did it start?) So argument between those with basically different even mutually unintelligible views does transpire. How? By self-correcting struggle to do what so many philosophers' arguments in principle declare to be impossible. Such as is modelled in this monograph.

Let me now develop relativism in its extreme epistemological form and show how it can be opposed and defeated by the concept of rationality I have proposed, a concept which is not ethnocentric but which draws on no more than the human abilities to learn from experience and to communicate.

The fundamental philosophical argument behind epistemological relativism is this. There is no way of mediating cross-cultural disagreement. If a conceptual system orders the world in a way different from the one we are used to, discussion between them will lead to a non-terminable disagreement.[8] To a westerner rice is rice, snow is snow, cows are cows; yet Asians can distinguish many kinds of rice, including some they feed only to animals but which we would eat, Eskimos distinguish many kinds of snow, and Nuer distinguish umpteen kinds of cow. Now, you can say, making such discriminations is a matter of training, like learning to 'hear' the tones in spoken Cantonese. It takes time, but the differences are there to be grasped. What, then, if your informants tell you that misfortune is due to witchcraft, and witchcraft is a substance detectable at a post-mortem examination of the body cavity? What if Aristotle tells you there is a passage between the left side and the right sides of the heart? What if someone tells you health and disease turn on a balance between hot and cold, dry and wet, yin and yang, strange and poisonous conditions?

We can cut open ever so many bodies and find no witchcraft substance and no hole in the heart and yet fail to convince believers. We can even develop an elaborate and quite successful alternative explanation of health and disease and find that it does not appeal to those convinced otherwise. The world really is the way we see it, then, and like the duck-rabbit drawing, or the protruding and recessive cube drawing, there is no correct exclusive way to see it.

Let us look at a highly sophisticated philosophical formulation of this, W. T. Jones's world-view relativism (Jones 1980). Jones notes the fact that persons have differing dispositions, both cognitive and attitudinal, and suggests ordering these differences on scales. Thus some of us may be very prejudiced towards foreigners, some of us less so, some of us indifferent, some of us quite positive about them, some of us warm and welcoming. These are attitudes, but a similar scale could be constructed of cognitive xenophobia-through-xenophilia. Jones discusses very general dimensions such as those involving a preference for the static rather than the changing, those preferring immediacy to distance, continuity to discreteness. Bias to one or other poles of such dimensions causes one to focus on features of experience ignored or minimized by those of different bias. Hence diametrically opposed theories may be developed.

Scrutinizing the metaphors and implicit assessments of Brand Blanshard's *Reason and Goodness*, Jones argues:

> a philosophical theory . . . reflects a pre-theoretical vision of the world . . . the vision renders the theory and the doctrine convincing – to those who share the vision. . . . From Hume's vision of reality the principle of induction cannot be defended; from Blanshard's, it cannot be challenged. Each is led to his conclusion by considerations that to him are irrefutable but to his opponent worthless. . . . This is one example of how a difference in world-view generates non-terminable disagreements. (p. 326)

Reflecting on possible challenges, he agrees that his view cannot be proved, because proof itself is a feature of, and relative to, a different world view (p. 330). And he then considers the self-refuting argument: that relativism 'absolutizes itself and thereby becomes incoherent' (p. 335). His answer is blunt:

> But world-view relativism relativizes relativism, and relativizes it to a particular world-view. An absolutized relativism argues for relativism and seeks to prove it. A relativized relativism eschews attempts to prove relativism, for it views argument and proof as relative to a particular world-view; they are part of the 'way of life' for which rationalists opt (p. 335).

This leads him to suggest that world-view relativism is not inconsistent – even though consistency as a value is a function of some world-views and not others.

The crucial question becomes, then, is change of world-view

possible, and if so how does it come about? Jones's view is that it does come about, but not by rational means, but rather by emotional means: shock treatment and therapy. Non-terminable disagreements are to be leaped not by argument or proof but by persuasion. This position itself, and all possible replies to it seem to Jones to presuppose the point at issue namely, do all views presuppose the point at issue?

Suppose, then, that Jones is right: that relativism can be consistently formulated so that it does not exempt itself and become incoherent. Must it then be embraced? Is it true, is it persuasive? Readers who have stayed with me so far will know that from my world-view there is no way I could agree to that. Indeed, I believe the enterprise of human intellectual endeavour is the articulation and criticism and hence improvement of world-views. Unlike Jones and Winch, I think there is a consistent meta-language where we can transcend world-view bias by discussing it. Jones's paper itself is in the meta-language and could not be written were it not available. To put it another way, the question 'is world-view relativism true?' can only be raised if it can be raised without presupposing an answer. If raising it presupposes an answer then it hasn't been raised and hence hasn't been answered.

But this tortuous reply is not really required, given Jones's formulation. All I need for my own claims is to say that, from the world-view I am stuck with, science is a universal and transcendent enterprise, that anthropology stems from that tradition, and hence appraisal, by anthropologists, of the cognitive and moral efforts of the people they study is intrinsic, presupposed. Anthropologists are using relativist arguments as a form of overkill. Not linking the actual judgments and views of their predecessors and some contemporaries such as Turnbull, they inconsistently maintain that all judgments are out of place. Hence it was possible for an high priest of relativism to be engaged in drafting for the United Nations a statement of Human Rights (Jarvie 1975a). But, a relativist must argue that whether humans have rights as well as what those rights are is world-view relative, and there are plenty of concrete differences observable on these matters in the world. So what authority can Herskovits or the UN assert in these matters?

Jones's argument is similar to Winch's and is one that has been seized on by religious apologists, who saw it as an unassailable defence in the warfare with science (White 1896). Instead of allowing that science and religion are competing cognitive systems, world-views which explain, in which science comes off best, they can treat each as a sort of culture, 'way of life', conceptual scheme, or domain sufficient unto itself, not in competition, not even in communication with each other. Religion and science become two different ways of life and thought and no clash between them is possible.

Evans-Pritchard would not buy this:

> It is an inevitable conclusion from Zande descriptions of witchcraft that it is not an objective reality. The physiological condition which is said to be the seat of witchcraft, and which I believe to be nothing more than food passing through the small intestine, is an objective condition, but the qualities they attribute to it and the rest of their beliefs about it are mystical. Witches, as Azande conceive them, cannot exist. (p. 63)

Ironically, it was from this passage that Peter Winch developed his ingenious version of radical relativism. Unlike Herskovits, Winch does not like to be called or thought of as a relativist.[9] Winch attempts to fuse Evans-Pritchards's grasp of the Azande world-view with the philosophy of the later Wittgenstein, to show that everything Evans-Pritchard says is in order, down to the point where he says that witchcraft is false. Winch argues that it makes no sense to say that there are no witches. For the Azande there are; their entire conception of the world embodies them. Forms of life have their rules, we cannot step outside and say the rules are wrong, for whose rules then govern our discourse? None? But then discourse would not be possible. The Azande don't worry about inconsistency, especially the inconsistency between witch-craft and apparent facts of the world. So, Winch says, what is true, what is rational, even what is logical will vary from culture to culture and no extra-cultural court of appeal exists to adjudicate differences.

Well, Evans-Pritchard thought there were no witches, and so do I. (Although not because they are mystical, and, also, I do not agree that they 'cannot' exist. They *can*; it is just that they don't.) In general, I think science, being super-rational, deserves credit for being nearer the truth than the world-view systems that preceded it. There is no way to turn base metals into gold, there is no influence of the stars on our lives, much disease is caused by the invasion of micro-organisms, not hexing; the fickle finger of fate distributes misfortune mostly by chance, and so on. More-over, we can argue the toss. It is not easy to argue these matters, but were it not possible, the progress of our own society from superstition and ignorance, to slightly less superstition and ignor-ance would be unintelligible, a non-rational process or conversion process, as Jones thinks it is. But a rational account of these changeovers is more plausible, is a better explanation than uncomprehending leaps from one world-view to another.

Gellner in *Legitimation of Belief* argues in effect that the kind of relativism promoted by Jones and Winch is true for all prescientific cognitive systems. They are incommensurable in details because there are deep divisions of underlying world-view that cannot be settled. As a bloc they are commensurable because of this similarity: they show little or no cognitive power, no self-starting ability to progress, no separation of cognitive activity from the rest of the social. A huge ditch separates those systems where cognition, pollution, taboo, religion, social status, kinship and so on are all mixed together, from the cognitive system we call 'science'. Gellner picks out four features of science that mark it off from systems on the other side of the Big Ditch. These are cognitive division of labour; no entrenched clauses; not judging in their own cause; and mechanism. They are a mixed bag but I have yet to come across a better negative set for characterizing the sorts of thought-systems science had to free itself from.

By the cognitive division of labour Gellner has in mind not the development of specialized expert roles or anything like that, but rather a doctrine about concepts. Since I am allergic to concepts, I shall talk about ideas. Translated to idea-talk, Gellner is saying that pre-scientific thought-systems use the same ideas for all sorts of purposes. An idea we might characterize as religious can also be used to cure illness, to predict eclipses or explain history. It is an enormous advance when this sort of wide use is overcome, and ideas are developed with precise domains of application.

By no entrenched clauses, Gellner is drawing attention to the way many pre-scientific belief-systems allow a degree of free-thought strictly circumscribed by certain entrenched ideas that cannot be challenged. The most obvious case would be certain deep-seated religious ideas that must not be challenged on pain of death. There may be subtler examples of abstract ideas so much part of the texture of thought that unthinking them is forbidden. A characteristic aim of the scientific world-view is to hold all questions open, allow all existing ideas to be challenged, to forbid entrenched clauses in the cognitive constitution. Boundaries of sacredness, pollution, centrality, ancientness, wide respect and so on, are all surmountable. Indeed, to the extent that science has deep roots in the questioning attitude of Socrates and Sextus, science virtually conceives it as a duty to challenge the received wisdom.

By ideas not being judges in their own cause Gellner has in mind something along these lines. Science depends upon replacing traditional or received means of adjudicating among ideas with means that are not themselves under the control of the possessors of those ideas, or of the ideas themselves. The analogy is in the attempt in legal systems to develop a court system of judge and jury that tries to determine the facts and apply the law *disinterestedly*. In practice this is very hard to do. It does not follow that it is impossible, or that because all attempts fall short to one or another degree, that all efforts to achieve the aim are equally futile. Similarly, while such notions as truth, reality and empiricism are full of philosophical troubles, the cognitive situation without even the attempt at them is much worse.

Finally mechanism. Here Gellner takes over a widely held characteristic of the scientific world-view, namely that it explains the natural world by natural means, and that these means are not extraordinary and depend upon mechanisms and processes that are in principle open to inspection by anyone. Scientists are not priests administering mysteries, despite occasional resemblances in their guild organization and enigmatic style of utterance. Science is an activity open to all who will master it, not surrounded in any essential way by initiation ritual, and taking pride in its claim to expose all its ideas and their backing to public scrutiny, both expert and lay. In a way, and here I go beyond Gellner – or back to Bacon – the mission of science is consciously democratic and egalitarian. Scientists aim to rethink our world-view and so in the long run have the aim of making discoveries available to all (Gellner 1973b, 1975, 1980).

This stringent and rather forbidding set of demands succeeded in bringing into being and sustaining a very powerful cognitive system, one qualitatively not just quantitatively different from all rivals and predecessors; one which was to make possible industrialization, secularization, affluence and liberation, which changed the character of life in society and of man's image of himself.

> current social thought is not in terms of transition *as such*, but of a *specific* transition: industrialisation (including, of course, modernisation of agriculture). . . . The most important thing about this transition is that it is one-way: beetle into man, but never man into beetle. To this extent, a non-differentiating relativism, extended to all *paths* as well [as] all *positions*, embracing all directions under an equalising cloak, simply cannot apply nowadays . . . societies can choose industrialism from a pre-industrial situation (and generally do when they have the choice) but not vice versa. . . . We may view traditional societies with nostalgia or disgust: be enchanted by their beauty, or revolted by their cruelty. It doesn't matter: they no longer present a viable alternative. . . . In other words,

107

we are here in the rather fortunate, and rather unusual, situation of knowing with practical certainty both that something will happen (though not just when and how) and that it is good. (Gellner 1964, pp. 68–9)

The picture this suggests is that our rationality leads us to take over from blind evolutionary mutations the problem of survival. Survival means food, water, shelter, protection from enemies, including disease. It means getting control over nature. Once this process has begun, other problems quickly surface to keep us busy, such as getting comfortable, having a high standard of living and so on. Nations and persons these days are not content to survive, they want to prosper. This seems to me eminently rational. Goal-directed action, problem-solving – rationality, in short – has given us the means to solve other problems than survival, indeed has made these other problems visible. That there is a rational and moral unity of mankind becomes apparent at this stage. The rationality manifests itself in communication and discussion about problems. The moral unity manifests itself in the selection of problems and the urgency given to them. Often enough any two given scientists will disagree on how a problem is to be solved; but they will agree to, and their rational unity transpires from, work on the problem. Similarly, often two moralists will disagree on what are the correct or best moral rules, but that they are needed and must be discussed they agree. Here is their unity.

Underlying a remark I made earlier about relativism having reasons behind it which we can't dismiss out of hand was this view: that the unity of mankind does not demand monolithic agreement – it requires open-minded discussion of what the problems are and how to go about solving them. Open-mindedness is both a rational (open to learning) and a moral (respectful) position, indeed only in such rationality can we find our moral unity.

3.3 The connection of weak absolutism with morality

Moralities, diverse moral ideas, are not just random collections. They are systems of rules and injunctions to live by. As such they are neither fixed nor given. They change over time and they differ from place to place, even person to person. The question is whether their changes and differences are random or systematic. My suggestion is that there is an element of system in their differences and this links up with the struggle for rationality: to learn the better to apply reason to tasks.

If the problem of morality is to devise rules for living together one may rank systems partly by how well they acknowledge this. An absolutist morality, for example, that sees morality as a question of obedience to the gods, of not committing sins – regardless of the degree to which this interferes with harmonious living – such a morality we may consider rather poorly adapted to the task. If the only reason for enforcing a taboo is that God has spoken against it, then that is saying little in defence of that taboo.

Obviously, what I have in mind is a purely secular conception of morality, just as we have a purely secular conception of cognition. This conception of morality we owe to Kant, who gave crystal clear reasons why we cannot pass the buck of morality on to some authority or other, human or divine. Since it is we who accept that morality and implement it, it is we who are unable to evade the responsibility. So morality is in the end traceable to down-to-earth human beings.

But I want to go much further than this and argue for the value of a secularized notion of morality because that is a rational system. Rationality, as we have discussed it in this monograph, comes down to the disposition and capacity to apply reason to tasks. The task of morality is devising rules, injunctions, prohibitions, prescriptions and so on that facilitate harmonious living in society. We may also add to the accomplishment of this task various other values besides harmony, such as individual freedom, equal moral treatment for all, minimum possible restrictions, and also, more dangerously, accordance with God's laws or, even more dangerous, the fostering of virtue and prevention of sin.

My conception of morality as a task to which we can apply reason is to view it as a means-ends matter: we set certain ends and morality tries to devise ways in which we can realize them. Thus it is indifferent at the first stage to what set of goals and values it is being devised to facilitate. This is not true of the second stage, as we shall see.

As in cognition, morality can be a rational learning process. The rules are a social institution in which many persons and their rational intelligences can participate. Morality is partly personal rules, partly it is embodied in what we call laws. In devising and revising laws we operate with a number of straightforwardly rational principles. It is important that laws be internally consistent and consistent with each other. It is important that the purposes of law be stated, so that their success can be estimated and their failure noted. A law prohibiting the sale and manufacture of alcoholic beverages may work or it may lead to their clandestine manufacture and the development of a large illegal traffic. The framers can then ask whether their campaign against alcohol might be better fought in the open. On marijuana no western country has yet had the courage to abolish prohibition; on prostitution, some countries make it clandestine, some have it in the open, carefully regulated. This is a rational or trial-and-error approach to law-making.

There is a perfect parallel with morality in general. Consider the question of honesty and of self-deception. Honesty is not merely a virtue because some religions say it is so; indeed, there are persuasive philosophical arguments to suggest that a society which lost the basic disposition to tell the truth could not function. So honesty is a crucial matter in the smooth working of life in society. What is the best way to promote it? Some people believe that all immorality should be heavily penalized. Sometimes this leads those who behave immorally to lie about it. They thus sin doubly. It may even lead to their behaving immorally and lying to themselves about it: consider lying in the name of their religion.

We need to discuss and learn from this about the best way to foster the virtues. We also learn to rank the virtues. Is sinning worse than lying about it, or is lying the worst sin, or perhaps self-deception? Depending on our answers to these questions we may, by practice and the instruction of our children, rely on somewhat different sets of moral rules.

Note that the process described is one of learning from experience. Because moral rules have no cognitive content does not mean we cannot learn anything about or from them. We can learn about their many consequences; we can learn about their consistency with other rules, practised and proposed; we can learn about their feasibility in practice. All this is knowledge, not of two times two equals four, or that masses attract each other with a force inversely proportional to the square of the distance between them, but *sui generis*: knowledge of morals. Not knowledge of The Good, but knowledge of the possibilities of life in human society.

What of the second level I spoke of? Well, I emphasized in the discussion of rationality that it is a reflexive process. That is, we learn not only about the world, we also learn about learning about the world. In so far as our methodological and sociological rules facilitate or hinder learning from experience, the growth of knowledge, we try to tinker with and add to them. It is a great advance, for example, to abandon attempts to formulate rules of inductive learning from both our philosophy of science and our scientific education. It is such a difficult task that although it was clearly preached by Bacon roughly three hundred and sixty years ago, it is still far from being accomplished.

Such reflexive rationality is relevant in morality too. Kant, for example, tried to argue that all moral concepts must be universalizable otherwise no moral inference could be validly drawn from them: this is important knowledge. We may discover that certain sorts of moral improvement are fostered by prohibition, others by relaxation. Freedom, for example, is not something that can be forced on people. Freedom is an absence, a minimum of rules both proscriptive and prescriptive. Similarly, the virtue of responsibility is promoted not by being enjoined, but by placing people in situations and leaving them to make mistakes and to learn. Parents can learn too that the promotion of morality in their children is partly a matter of example, partly of explicit teaching, but also has much to do with a judicious mixture of the freedom to learn by making mistakes. No recipes exist, though.

Perhaps the greatest set of lessons to be learned in the field of morals, however, is to do with the system of goals and virtues we want to promote. Freedom of thought, speech and action, for example, is widely touted as a virtue of a society. Less widely touted is the way this virtue forces us to downgrade certain other virtues in the moral ordering if we are to be consistent. For example, it entails that no world religion can be promoted as a top priority. The founders of the United States knew this when they enjoined no establishment of religion. To this day there are pressures from religious groups to enshrine their moral ideas in the law and the schools and the mass media. This is done with lip-service to the morality of freedom. What should be being learned here is the inconsistency between simultaneously pursued goals.

Our record on this team-learning about morality is very dismal. The reason is perhaps plain. Decidophobia: reluctance to take responsibility. Most systems of morality are authoritarian. To acknowledge Kant's point that this is an evasion amounts to accepting personal responsibility and hence accountability for moral actions, rules and consequences. Aversion to this is deep-seated indeed. The law is a little better in most western countries, although it is still not treated pragmatically enough as a social device to achieve goals rather than a sacred cow, a buttress against chaos and immorality. We have much to learn in the process of learning about morality. Moral disputes, also, are either related back to authorities, a move that is logically invalid, or they are relativized. And this brings us back to our basic topic, which is diversity and relativism.

Anthropologists do not sufficiently acknowledge the depths of Durkheim's idea that transcendental systems are the social system writ large. Local moralities, and local moral diversity are at best expression of the wisdom of the locals. The wisdom of the locals doesn't usually even encompass, still less does it offer a solution to the problem of the diversity of moral ideas between localities. The anthropologist, the professional comparer of localities, abrogates all pretence to rational learning when he becomes a relativist because he is assuming that there is no learning possible in regard to the tasks the different moralities face. To take a simple and graphic couple of examples: if a society has a morality that permits, indeed endorses, infanticide or geronticide and clearly that is related to the aim of minimizing unproductive mouths in an infertile environment, why should not the anthropologist allow that contraception on the one hand and social security on the other may be better ways of dealing with the achieving of the same aims? Why better? Because, let us assume, the human individual and his/her life has the same value set upon it as in societies we are familiar with. Then, the inconsistency involved in excusing or endorsing infanticide and geronticide can be eliminated by contraception and social security. Of course, neither contraception nor social security can be introduced into tribal society. A level of affluence probably derived from industrialization or at least a wage economy tied to other countries' industrialization is necessary, also a governmental and educational infrastructure such that government, taxation and planning are sufficient to run a social security system, also a level of education sufficient to understand and use contraception. And all of this presupposing that neither involves direct clash with religious injunctions.

Anthropologists used to undertake the task of developing a rational morality. But that failed because of their limited and excessively strong notion of rationality as ideas all rational men agree on. There are not and never will be such things. There are no unassailable moral principles immune for ever to criticism and improvement. Morality is like science where we assume as a matter of course that all current theory will be overthrown, and stability will come from its being incorporated to a certain extent in new and all-embracing ideas. Rational morality is not atheism plus the felicity calculus. Rationality is not consensus. Rationality is best understood as applying reason to tasks, the rational anthropologist is then contemplating the task of making sense of other societies in the first instance. But in the second instance the anthropologist is trying to make intra-societal sense of human efforts to live together. To stand back and wave his hands in wonder at the diversity of man's social works is all very well, but then comes the hard part. Is it really equally wonderful to be sunk in poverty and superstition as in enlightenment, affluence and progress? Is it really equally wonderful to kill off surplus children or useless old people, as it is to space children? Are all systems of the distribution of wealth equally good? And so on.

No simple-minded unlinear evolutionary scheme need be the outcome of such thinking, but some sort of ranking, some sort of evidence of the possibility of human societies learning from one another and about themselves is surely demanded.

Epilogue

Anthropology and socio-cultural transcendence

E.1 Reflections

A few years ago I was asked to read the manuscript of a book of papers reflecting on the anthropological experience of studying religious cults (which became *Social Research* 1979). This provoked me to reflect on my own experience with the cult of anthropology and to reflect back on the nature of the encounter between the observer and the observed. At the end I tried to sum up my vision of the anthropological enterprise as a humane, scientific and progressive endeavour.

Reading anthropologists' reflections on their contact with religious movements, and on their former selves, it was striking how two themes persisted. One was *encounter* between the self and others (anthropology), and between the self and the former self (anthropologists). The other was *commitment*, whether to anthropology as a humane enterprise, to one's self, or to the people studied. Encounter, it seems, is always a threat to commitment: it is not easy to maintain one's commitments in alien surroundings; the ways of alien people have a way of challenging the assumptions one may not even have noticed one was committed to. Encounter with the dark forces can be so harrowing that the anthropologist may be repulsed; or may convert; or may come to look at anthropology as itself a form of social and cultural adaptation to a changing world, a form of cult or magic itself; that the anthropologist is like the prophets and magicians he studies, using the dreams, fears and desires of the culture in the presentation of their message.[1]

Though encounter has this effect on commitment we still seek it: this might seem ordinary enough: encounter is a part of our experience, and we all hope to learn from experience. Yet two things are worth noting here as rather extraordinary. One is that commitments are often taken to be just those things on which we predicate our learning; not at all the sorts of things it is possible for us to chop and change in the course of learning and under the impact of new experiences. Commitments are usually thought to lie behind a protective belt of epistemological and psychological devices that prevent experience inflicting any damage on them.[2] Yet George Orwell noted (*Clergyman's Daughter*) that commitments come and go and cannot be kept; that their changes are somehow linked with experience, with encounter. The other point is that among the commitments being challenged here are not just first order but also the meta-commitments – commitments, that is, to this or that tradition of enquiry.

One might not normally expect that experience would penetrate the protective belt and affect both commitments and meta-commitments. For if and when it does so, it invalidates commitments as the (unquestioned) *grounds* of enquiry, and for logical reasons. That is to say, if facts can threaten commitment, this suffices to deprive it of its ascribed foundational status. So: either the protective belt does its job unfailingly; or, other grounds for enquiry must be sought. A third conclusion is possible: enquiry needs no grounds; presuppositions are always only for the sake of argument and can at will become themselves subject to further argument. Such a third alternative is one that I have explored for many years trying to draw the consequences it appears to have for anthropological enquiry.

The clash between encounter and deep commitment or meta-commitment is one that I can hardly but welcome. In my first book I tried to show how cargo cults, or rather, the attempts of anthropologists to grapple with cargo cults, could tell us something about anthropology itself.[3] There seemed to me to be deeply buried philosophical commitments in anthropology that cargo cults could show up to be the prejudices that they were: inductivism, sensationalism, and essentialism were among those I picked out. It was and is my view that there are no commitments so deep as to be unreachable. Everything is negotiable with experience, including the notions of experience and of the objects of experience. In a way, precisely such negotiation is what (western) philosophy is.[4] So, it is not unexpected that anthropologists, prepared to follow the argument wherever it leads, might detect a clash between their field experience and the endeavour which brought them to the field in the first place – attraction or repulsion.

The question I want now to pose is whether they should take the further step of concluding that it is not commitments that yield to experience, but the principle of commitment itself, the idea

ANTHROPOLOGY AND SOCIO-CULTURAL TRANSCENDENCE

that commitment is the foundation of all experience. The step, that is, of arguing that once one's commitments have been shaken, one can no longer settle as comfortably into new commitments as before. For once shaken, commitments no longer have that feeling of being entrenched clauses, out of reach, lived by rather than intellectualized.[5] The commitment to a way of doing anthropology leads to discoveries that shake the commitment to anthropology itself, and that in turn shakes confidence in commitment itself. Or does it?

My hesitation stems from a remark of Bernadetta Jules-Rosette (1978), which I say frankly, quite took me aback. The diviner John Marinke asks her: 'Are you skeptical of African science?' *And she shakes her head*. This is in the course of an absorbing and sensitive paper that repudiates romanticism, and strives (wo)manfully to regain the enterprise of science. She has it that in the end whatever understanding the anthropologist has gained must be translated back into the language of social science.

Why am I taken aback? Because I take the oxymoron 'committed science' to be in fact a contradiction in terms.[6] It would seem to me incumbent upon anyone purporting to be a social scientist to answer the question with a nod of the head. (Perhaps adding a disclaimer like. 'And also of many other things.'[7]) And here I find it terribly hard to disentangle my own personal scepticism from the sceptical attitude I feel to be a deep part of science, especially science that has been engaged in self-reflection.[8] If I was studying the arcana of nuclear physics or medicine and was asked whether I was sceptical of western science, I am afraid I should nod my head as vigorously as I would were I asked the same question about Uri Geller. John Marinke is not Uri Geller and Bernadetta Jules-Rosette is not ICJ.

Scepticism, I would hazard, is a mandatory part of the scientific attitude, because only scepticism allows one to be ruthlessly critical not only of the ideas of others, but, more especially, of one's own pet ideas. The very thought of being unsceptical towards African science gives me vertigo. Scientists – anthropologists included – are, or should be, *professional* sceptics. They are reporters, commentators, on the human condition; a condition in which they participate, of course. But they are not reporting on those aspects of it in which they participate with all men, they are reporting on those aspects of it which seem different, alien, exotic, inexplicable, irrational. They are professionally marginal men. It is often remarked that the sorts of people who become sociologists and anthropologists are people marginal to their society: outsiders, immigrants, members of minorities, etc., and that the social sciences as it were rationalize their situation. Perhaps so. Social science might also be seen as the struggle to become marginal; the effort to differentiate oneself from the rest of mankind; to free oneself from the assumptions and preconceptions other men take for granted, live by; the attempt to transcend one's society in order the more clearly to see it and oneself. Social understanding does not mean one ceases to be a social being: that is impossible. Similarly, self-understanding does not imply that one ceases to be a self. What one endeavours to do is to achieve distance from one's society, to achieve distance from one's fellow man, ultimately, to achieve distance from oneself. This distancing, which we already experience unreflectively in what we call self-consciousness, and which ethnomethodologists achieve by 'throwing',[9] is very hard to achieve, and even harder to maintain. There are those who question its value or its legitimacy. My argument would be that there is no going back now: it is rather like being naive or unself-conscious; once one has lost those pristine states, they are gone forever. Social naïveté and unself-consciousness went out long before the Greeks. Men have been able to view themselves and their social arrangements with detachment at least since then. Given that there is no going back, no lost community of self, society and fellowship that we can regain, the most rational policy is to try to do the job well.

Part of the problem here has to do with commitment. If we could get rid of commitment, that is, if we could get rid of the commitment to commitment, the anthropology of religious experience might be more progressive, we might learn from encounter more than we now do. Far too many anthropologists take religion suspiciously seriously. When I say 'suspiciously', what I am suspicious of is that they may themselves be believers, or former believers, who remain committed to the view that religion is an authentic experience to which the anthropologist must do justice, pay due respect, etc., and take this pretext to be commitment to scientific anthropology. Thus, in a classic case, Evans-Pritchard is scathing about Durkheim's views on religion, when one suspects this is because Durkheim is not committed to religion, is neither attracted nor repelled. Perhaps this is a problem that will never be solved, for it arises in philosophy as well as anthropology: the problem, namely, of whether or not one should allow oneself to be committed to religion. Not to this or that specific religion, but to religion as such or in general. Committed to religion or to the religion of anti-religion, anthropologists undergo an encounter which makes them change or modify self and commitment, including commitment to self. Were they from the start more professionally or methodologically sceptical – of themselves, of science, of anthropology, certainly of religion, of all human activity – cognitive as well as behavioural – perhaps their unease would be lessened. But their aim to preserve commitment affects their habit or methodology. This is as it should be, of course, for recommendations about methods turn on views of aims. I therefore think we need to discuss the aims of anthropology. A standard view is that anthropology aims to describe. This aim can be criticized as inadequate since it does not specify what is to be described, and because an argument can be made that everything can be described in infinitely many different ways. Another view is that anthropology aims to explain why people do things. This seems to be a misunderstanding. Freud may tell us why we do things, but subjects like anthropology, sociology and economics concentrate instead on the consequences of the fact that we simply do do things (Hayek 1953, p. 39). My present view (1972b) is that the social sciences aim to explain what might be called the unintended consequences of people's actions; and I follow Popper in holding that anthropology is best regarded as the general, cross-cultural form of sociology.[10] Take automobile accidents. The social scientist's aim is not to explain automobile accidents, unless they are true accidents, when we seek those unintended aspects of the physical and human situation that brought them about (bad weather, poor signs, distractions, etc.); otherwise, the reasons road-signing is poor, or the reasons the driver is distracted or drunk, what one might call the causes of the accident, are the purview of applied rather than theoretical social science. Rather, theorists concern themselves with things like markets, kinship systems, land tenure, political arrangements, religious ceremonies, and the like. Malinowski on the *kula*, Mauss on the potlatch, Durkheim on the elementary forms, Evans-Pritchard on the Nuer lineage and feud, Radcliffe-Brown on Australian marriage rules, Fortes on Tallensi kinship, etc., all these great anthropologists were exploring the unintended consequences, the systemic outcome, of the actions of actors. To adapt the immortal phrase of Adam Ferguson, the results of human action, but not the execution of any human design. Because no human design is involved, such results, outcomes, systems, are problematic, require explanation. Or, to be more precise, many will be taken for granted, even unnoticed. It is when some theory goes wrong, when human design is thwarted, that we notice the gap in our understanding of our own social system. An anthropologist merely magnifies this. He finds almost the entire system he is endeavouring to enter problematic, the more so as his efforts to enter it are thwarted. From this encounter, anthropology stems; this encounter is the individual microcosm of the global and persistent

121

phenomenon of culture contact and culture clash, which may be the engine of all intellectual and cultural progress.

Problemstellung, which can by no means be taken for granted, can be seen as contrasted with, even opposed to, a different aim, one so diffuse it is hard to formulate, but one might caricature and call it 'acting out one's love for mankind', and hence stressing empathy, *engagement*, understanding, mutual interaction, shared reality production, and the like. All this is very moral and very earnest. One might ask what it is all for? What problems is it supposed to solve? The problem perhaps of human misunderstanding, or lack of communication? If this, then I would argue it is both misconceived and naive. No class of mediators is needed to cope with the problem of communication. Nations and societies can communicate through their diplomats, their interpreters, travellers, etc. There is no point in financing people to go on expensive expeditions to the ends of the earth to gratify a yearning for empathy with their fellowman, or to chisel away at problems of human communication. The naïveté is to think of the problem of communication as a specifiable and hence solvable problem like the problem of whether to grant diplomatic immunity. Communication problems, even within the same culture, the same family, are a part of the human condition with which we all continually struggle, but which can hardly legitimate a specific academic endeavour like anthropology.

My view is, I acknowledge, an intellectualist view. And I note how few allies I have in anthropology. The ordeal-by-fieldwork has been replaced by fieldwork-as-personal-odyssey-and-self-discovery. So I find myself in the awkward position of speaking for the older anthropological tradition, which concerns not the doer but the deeds. Following that tradition I ask, 'What problems have we solved, with what theories, to which tests have they been put, and to which further ones should they be put?'

One might compare the situation, as Jules-Rosette does, to the learning of a language. One reason to learn the language of a faraway place might be that one wants to go and live there. This is rather an odd aim if one has never been there; but never mind. Another reason might be that one wants to learn the language in order to be able to translate from that language back into one's own, to tell people things. This is a public purpose, to which the method of total immersion, empathy, etc., may be appropriate, as may many other methods, including course-work and private study. In the first case the end is private. If you don't wish to bring them to us (or us to them, as medical missionary, e.g.) then the purpose is private and of no legitimate intellectual or academic concern. Empathy may be all right as a moral or methodological stance, but it is not itself sufficient.

Jules-Rosette says that unless this translation back is accomplished then why call the result of one's endeavours science? This is too weak. What needs to be said is that science has presuppositions – among them a basic realism. Realism has notoriously many philosophical difficulties, as has a realistic empiricism. Bishop Berkeley thought that that showed one had to retreat into idealistic phenomenalism (Wisdom 1953, pp. 1–80). This is a mistake. Phenomenalism and idealism have even more notorious difficulties. That the basis of science is realistic, more so in the social sciences, seems to be blindingly obvious. We do not allow the problem of other minds to drive us into solipsism; no more should we allow arguments from the social construction of reality to drive us away from realism (Wisdom 1973). For all the difficulties of realism, it still has obvious and very powerful arguments in its favour, including those from evolution.

Having come so far, and having focussed the issue in philosophical terms, I now turn to a brief autobiographical offering.

E.2 Recollections

By profession, I am a philosopher of science. I teach in a philosophy department and am without formal standing among social scientists.[11] My BScEcon was in social anthropology, but my PhD, also within the Faculty of Economics, is in scientific method. This, I suppose, makes me an officially certified methodologist. Anyway, whatever I am, or take myself to be, I seem to be a stranger or outsider to anthropologists.[12] Especially when their concern is reflections on their field experience, and their estimate of the impact it has had upon themselves and their ideas. However, I have long been struggling with my own fieldwork and conversion experience. The experience in question was with a secular cult known as British social anthropology.[13] Unlike some anthropologists, my struggle was to *avoid* conversion, to refuse assent to the community, to stay marginal, to insist on accepting only what I chose. To avoid attraction and repulsion. It was in this posture that I commenced my research into cargo cults twenty-five years ago. My desire to do a philosophical-cum-methodological PhD thesis in the library, rather than an anthropological-fieldwork one, was an expression of my resistance to conversion to anthropology, whose high priests at that time considered fieldwork mandatory.[14] I had no desire whatever to do fieldwork, even in a remote part of Britain as was then fashionable, as I imagined it to be a form of brainwashing, an irrational condition.

It was a blow to me when my mentor, the late lamented Maurice Freedman, told me that my philosophical methodological research proposal was unacceptable to the anthropologists even though he had kindly passed it on to the philosophers. They, it turned out, were very willing to help me develop my ideas, and so I became a student of philosophy quite despite myself. This crisis of identity has never been resolved, and I have learned to exploit the status of a marginal man: to play philosopher to anthropologists, anthropologist to philosophers; to exploit an intellectual niche, whether it be called interdisciplinary studies, philosophy of the social sciences, or methodology.

In the course of developing my critique of social anthropology, under the auspices of philosophy, a critique which could fairly be described as my apologia for not converting, I decided that cargo cults, being weird but fascinating, might give me a clue as to why conversion was not for me. Unexpectedly, the harvest was very great. These cults taught me to de-ethnocentrize myself (so far from being weird and bizarre, they approximate closely to the religious norm of much of the world over much of recorded time), and to see the institutionalized religion of my native Britain as the exception not the norm. They also taught me that the anthropology of anthropology, indeed the anthropology of the intellectual world, was a rich seam which could be mined for many years to come.

Religion, I confess always had been rather distasteful to me. Virtually my only background was the diffused Protestantism of secular British culture (school hymns and prayers, public ceremonies, etc.). From early adolescence I had decided the arguments for agnosticism, at the very least, were overwhelming.[15] Later on, however, my resistance to conversion became stronger, perhaps because of my tussle with social anthropology, and I concluded that the utter absurdity of religious beliefs and practices forced me to be atheistic.[16]

Omitted from these autobiographical comments so far is my encounter with the system of ideas to which I do attach myself, a unique system of ideas that does not demand, indeed discourages, conversion; does not articulate and defend particular beliefs, but encourages a certain policy towards all beliefs. This is the philosophy of Karl Popper. As indicated, I had already developed something of a sceptical temperament where it came to attachment to systems of ideas. In my first year at the London School of Economics, I took logic and scientific method under Popper. After that, I thought no more about him for a while, until I began to miss the critical stimulation of his lectures. This was during my second year. So, as a substitute (he gave no second- or third-year lectures in those days), I decided to read *The Open Society and Its Enemies* – the only book of his then available in English. This must have been in the spring of 1957. Here suddenly was a coherent articulation of my scepticism; here was a critical philosophy which explained to me why I resisted intellectual conversion experiences, whether studying economics or social anthropology. Soon after, I decided to take my honours degree in anthropology, and requested permission, as a senior undergraduate, to sit in on Popper's graduate seminar. This was granted. That seminar, which I attended regularly for the next four-and-a-half years, gave me completely new aspirations in the world of ideas. It was an institution in which diverse people came together to reason about all sorts of topics. Research students and visiting academics from diverse fields came and aired their latest ideas for critical scrutiny. In practice, Popper's philosophy consisted of no more than the endeavour to carry these explorations forward with the utmost vigour and rigour. Some people could not stand this; their open-mindedness and critical attitude had limits. Religion, I soon realized, was often at the root of the trouble, since it meant taking some ideas for granted, rendering some immune from scrutiny. Limits of open-mindedness seemed intellectually indefensible, yet I began to detect something like them at work in social anthropology. Social anthropology was not just a field or a method, it seemed like a system of methodological and substantial ideas which the student was expected to swallow. This indeed, is how Polanyi and Kuhn have since described science (Polanyi 1958; Kuhn 1962).

Hence, when I was passed on to the philosophers as a research student, I was able almost immediately to settle down to my main problem: disentangling the open- and closed-minded aspects of anthropology. I took as my case study, disentangling the open- and closed-minded aspects of Melanesian thinking as embodied in their cargo cults, and of anthropologists as embodied in their thinking about cargo cults.

Where did all this leave me? Rather distant from the anthropological commitment. A sceptic and a marginal man who very much wanted to remain one, and did not secretly admire or yearn for the security of a lost faith or lost community. Someone not prepared to be more charitable to the religious ideas and systems of native peoples than he was to the religious ideas and systems of his own people. Hence, when Jules-Rosette is asked whether she believes in African science, she replies yes; and proceeds to be initiated. I had in effect been asked whether I believed in social anthropology and had replied 'no'; so my initiation was strictly circumscribed. That was fine by me. If someone asks me whether

I believe in western science, Chinese science, or African science, my answer is 'no'. As E. M. Forster said, 'I don't believe in belief'.[17] Belief takes away from me a distance, a scepticism, a reservation, which I want always to have, and which I think is essential to intellectual integrity.[18]

Coming, then, to the literature on cargo cults was a bit like coming to any ancient or remote text. All sorts of error and nonsense would likely be buried there, but this was not my main concern. Starting from a sceptical point of view, I did not feel that it was false or nonsensical ideas that needed explanation; it seemed to me that all ideas were in need of explanation. Perhaps we have made a little progress in the small realm of scientific ideas; however, that was a debatable matter, and the debate itself highlighted the precariousness and need of explanation of even such minimal claims. Rather, the problem seemed to me to be to employ imagination and insight in a manner that would make sense of the cargo cults whilst preserving the apparent falseness, even absurdity, of some of their ideas. Neither attraction nor repulsion. Surrounded in my own society by committed people, I felt only the greatest respect for the sceptical overturning of religious theories of the world that cargo cultists seemed to go in for.

As I struggled to understand cargo cults, and anthropologists' understanding of cargo cults, I seemed to see a pattern at work. In remote Melanesia, the eruption of culture contact created an intellectual problem: what is going on? Cargo cult doctrines, garbled, confused and syncretic as they were, made sense as conjectures intended to explain what was going on, and rectify what was perceived as a worsening or intolerable state of affairs (Burridge 1960, 1969a, Cochrane 1970). That their ideas were tied to specific expectations at specific times had the disadvantage that the cult might collapse,[19] and the advantage that error would be exposed. (Note how rationalist or intellectualist I was being.)[20] Such an idea had escaped most anthropologists, who had instead displayed their bafflement by the bewildering array of putative explanations of the cults they offered: stupidity, psychological derangement, irrationality, lack of contact with reality, nativism, oppression, class struggle and so on.[21] Yet I could see pretty clearly that much more research was needed.

Soon after my book appeared, Peter Lawrence's masterpiece *Road Belong Cargo* (1964) came to hand, carrying out a programme very close to what I had thought necessary. Little remained for me to do but hail it, analyse it, and note that even in their character as cults, cargo cults were part of a traditional Melanesian mode of response (1968).

But anthropologists were not prepared to come out and debate the issues. Instead, in classic religious or dogmatic school fashion, they closed ranks, made surreptitious changes and modifications, watered down their ideas, and chased hares and fads (structuralism, network theory) (see my 1975b). Anthropology is like a craft guild, insisting on its master-apprentice initiation through fieldwork, but trading in uncommunicable mysteries, *Personal Knowledge*, as Polanyi called it.[22] This I felt to be explicable only by taking quite literally the idea that they were a tribe held together by a cult, an ancestral-cum-cargo cult. The religion was the tribe. Festinger et al. (1956) predicted that disappointed cultists retreat in on themselves and present a brave face to the world. They then attempt to reduce dissonance by further proselytizing. This certainly seems to have happened in anthropology. Sceptics and wreckers are shoved aside, and the subject tramps on, going nowhere, whistling noisily to keep its spirits up.

When I say this, I speak of anthropology conceived of as an attempt to understand and hence come to terms with the human condition.[23] On these matters the subject is not progressing satisfactorily. Exploring cults is also self-exploration; understanding cults can increase self-understanding. They can, indeed, increase our understanding of the academic role itself.

E.3 Lessons

My argument so far has been that my encounter with cargo cult religion led me to sociological discoveries: to spotting parallels between the study of an ostensibly 'academic' subject like anthropology, and millenarian religion. This involves not taking academic subjects altogether seriously at *their* face value either.[24] The parallel has its limitations, no doubt, but it also has hidden strengths. For example, I found that when bringing my thinking up to date in a more recent paper, it felt a bit like writing an epistle (1975). What I had not seen, although it now seems clear enough, was that the parallel can be generalized. I was brought to see this not by reading social scientists, but by reading a novel, one which I propose now to describe and discuss.

Alison Lurie has written a series of novels about academic and intellectual life, among the most brilliant of which is *Imaginary Friends*.[25] This is relevant here simply because it is about the study of a small millenarian cult in upstate New York. The protagonists, besides the cultists themselves, are two university professors; one very young and in his first job, the other middle-aged and securely established as the author of a sociological classic, since when he has not published much. Upstate New York is not far from Cornell, where Ms Lurie teaches, and has for long been an area of intense fringe religious activity. Otherwise, much of the general scheme of the cult has obviously come from reading Festinger's *When Prophecy Fails*.

What the novel does that I had not seen and which illuminates the theme of this volume is simple enough. It shows how the presuppositions of a sociological enterprise like this doom it from the start: the sociologist would dearly love to be invisible, but cannot hope to be; the sociologist wishes to be immune and aloof, self-contained and untouched, but he cannot be; the sociologist is either attracted or repelled, and both lead to disaster. The study of the cult affects the cult and, more significantly, affects those who study it. McMann the older professor, ends up straddling the border between madness and sanity. The hubris of trying to be god and man at the same time, student and creator, human and super-human, sane and mad, attracted and repelled becomes manifest in McMann. Zimmern, the younger investigator, only just manages to cope and somehow salvage his career. Yet he is unable to understand what has happened; not what went wrong, but what is wrong. Ms Lurie's novel challenges the very enterprise of studying people in society.

Roger Zimmern, an untenured young professor, stands in awe of Thomas McMann, author of the sociological classic, *We and They: Role Conflict in River City*. However, a bond grows between them, and McMann proposes they engage in a joint study of a small cult in the nearby town of Sophis. It transpires that a small group there called the Truth Seekers, meets in the home of middle-aged Mrs Elsie Novar, where resides also a nineteen-year-old medium called Verena Roberts. Verena has received messages ostensibly from a distant planet, Varna, and its leader, Ro.

The group is quite small, eight or ten people, and both small town and kin. Commuting from the university, Roger and Tom pretend to be itinerant businessmen, although this pretence is later exposed and dropped. Soon after their joining, the group becomes more intense, and a date is set for the arrival of the space men. Rituals are enacted, including dietary and clothing prohibitions. When the prophecy fails to be fulfilled Verena concludes that Ro *has* arrived and entered all of them, and that now life can return to normal. Elsie, however, struggling to interpret the 'message', concludes that Ro has entered Professor Tom McMann who now is Ro of Varna.

At this point, Verena's boyfriend tries to take her away, and is himself driven away by Tom, who accuses him of being in league with jealous academic colleagues out to sabotage his study. Ken returns with the police, and McMann resists. In the final scene, Roger visits McMann in the asylum, where the latter maintains that he is playing at being mad in order to do another sociological project. Moreover, he continues, when he gets out, he intends to lead the group forward into a mass movement. Roger's doubts enrage McMann and he chases him away.

So much for summary. Among the fascinating aspects of the novel are how, for example, the two academic strangers give additional weight to the group, the more so after it is discovered that they are among the despised professoriate. It illustrates the virtual impossibility of sticking to non-directive responses to everything. Roger is very conscientious about this, and as a result becomes the kind of group idiot. McMann, bluff and confident, constantly sails close to the wind, justifying himself in relation to The Study. Allegory, too, is used. The group is called the Truth Seekers, and they meet near a small college town. Explicit parallels are drawn with the University:

> The Seekers didn't seem any less crazy, but now everyone else, especially my students, was starting to resemble them. Essentially, they were all converts to the same religion, or victims of the same illusion: they believed in education, in science, in the voice of authority. (p. 60)

As the time of The Coming approaches:

> The Seekers had lectures, they had readings in approved texts, they had assignments (twenty minutes of meditation on set topics before breakfast every day, short essays on matters of special interest). They were expected to take notes at meetings, and copy out the messages received. Between times, they had to study the 'lessons' and memorize the prayers, lists, and definitions dictated by Ro and his friends, preparing themselves to be questioned on them at any time: in effect, called on to recite in class. . . . The whole thing got to be like a relentless parody of higher education. There was the same intense seriousness about a body of accumulating data which was, to say the least, unverifiable; the same assumption that here was a small group of enlightened, thinking persons who understood the universe correctly. As for the messages from Varna, aren't articles in most professional journals a form of automatic writing? It is another self who speaks there, solemn and oracular, in a cryptic jargon the real man would never use. (p. 110)

Just before The Coming, talking over the plan with McMann:

> I saw something else too: a connection between McMann's hypothesis about the Truth Seekers and his position in the

129

Department, even in the world. Opposition would never shake his own convictions, so he wanted and expected the Seekers to hold to theirs. (p. 184)

Earlier on, when Roger expresses concern about Verena not eating:

'Listen Verena may look pathetic to you,' he said in his seminar manner, bluff but highly educated. 'But she can take care of herself. You've got to remember, that girl has already changed a number of people's lives rather profoundly. Elsie, Milly, Rufus, the whole lot of them. Don't let her fool you. . . .' There were two more lives Verena had changed, I thought, that McMann had overlooked: his and mine. (p. 115)

My reasons for bringing up this novel, rather than say some field encounter, should now be fairly obvious. It is true the fieldwork experience has a deep effect on those in it, emotionally, morally and cognitively. It is also true that the endeavours of cultists have great similarities to doing sociology. Moreover it seems that education itself, perhaps especially autonomous higher education, is similar too. This seems to show that there is something universal in the experience of encounter: encounter with new people, new groups, and also encounter with new ideas, dark forces. Since, except for the solitary scholar, most encounters of this kind take place in a social context, where new people, new groups and new ideas are all encountered together, it should cease to surprise us that the encounter with the religious cults of remote peoples has had such an effect on anthropologists and anthropology. Religious experience is after all that place in most societies where individual, group and cognitive encounter are found most frequently and most intensely. In everyday work people are frequently scattered and busy. But at the times of ceremony, rites, religious meetings, etc., they engage with each other and with ideas in their most general form and are attracted or repelled.

Nevertheless, to generalize further, I continue to be impressed by the everyday character of the struggle to be curious and sceptical, not attracted or repelled. Entering a new town, a new university, every term a new classroom, always seems to me to involve these elements, and hence always, to a degree, to affect one cognitively as well as emotionally. Ms Lurie may intend her allegory as a criticism of social science. I do not take it as such. I take it that all human encounter is self-making, and human encounter with the ideas and attitudes of others can be self-transcending. But this is an arduous and precarious endeavour

130

that can leave us disillusioned or mad, as easily as enlightened and renewed.

Notes

Prologue

1 *New York Times*. 3 January 1971, p. 46: 'Survival Shocks Apocalyptic Sect'; *Kitchener-Waterloo Record*, 20 October 1971, p. 30: 'Cargo Cultists Think Rituals Bring Gifts'; *Los Angeles Times*, 29 June 1981, Part II, p. 3: 'Sect Waits All Day to be Lifted Heavenward'.

2 Even now its history remains to be written. Recent attempts such as Kuper (1973) and Langham (1981) offer disparate pictures and use diverse sources.

3 Agassi (1963, pp. 1–3) calls it 'up-to-date-science-textbook-worship' for short.

4 Or, rather, they are the only histories of the academic subject. Many excellent historians of ideas have written about topics in metaphysical anthropology such as Bury (1932), Lovejoy (1936), Lovejoy and Boas (1935), Pearce (1953), Hanke (1949, 1959, 1974), Popkin, (1974a and b, 1978), Gossett (1963), Fredrickson (1971), Huddleston (1967), Bolt (1971), Curtin (1964), Jordan (1968), Sheehan (1980), Elliott (1972), O'Gorman (1961), Stepan (1982). These names are mostly absent from Tax (1955), Eggan (1969), Lowie (1937), Kuper (1973), not to mention Evans-Pritchard (1981), Freedman (1978), Honigman (1976), Leaf (1979) and Maalefit (1974).

5 See Agassi (1959), Burtt (1925) and, on problem co-ordination, Agassi (1964).

6 See Stoddard (1920, 1923, 1924, 1926, 1927, 1935, 1940).

7 The controversy about Coon is in *Current Anthropology*, vol. 4, 1963, 360–67 and, vol. 5, 1964, 313–20; the literature on Jensen is in Eysenck (1981); see also Stepan (1982. ch. 7).

8 While one contradictory statement is enough to refute, no amount of verifying statements confirm. This logical asymmetry of falsification and verification is fundamental in methodology and widely ignored or misunderstood.

The conception of metaphysics with which I am operating, namely, doctrines that can be verified but not falsified, is due to Popper 1959. It was effectively popularized by Watkins (1957, 1958, 1960), although his characterization of it is in error (Popper 1983).

9 The significance of the British formula (racialism+indirect rule) versus the French formula (assimilationism+direct rule) is unclear. The British did not offer British culture and civilization to the locals in quite the same way. Their schoolchildren did not learn 'nos ancestres les gaulois'.

Part one Rationality

1 Although everyone knows that Aristotle says that man is the rational animal, in fact the phrase is a gloss and nowhere appears quite like that in the corpus of his works. The nearest I can find is 1421a11. cf. Baldry (1965).

2 See Michael Haynes, 'Evolution and Language: A critique of Linguistic Innatism', PhD Dissertation, York University, Toronto 1983, unpublished; also Hattiangadi and Ziv (1982).

3 This reading of Bacon is a conscious attempt to show how appreciation of him is bedevilled by his theory of induction, a particular cashing out of his general approach to rationality that is severely deficient while yet more sophisticated than most subsequent attempts. He only fails to be included among the canonical philosophers because Hegel, when inventing the subject of philosophy by writing its history, excluded him because he did not have a system. Yet Urbach's (1982) attempt to treat Bacon as a precursor of Popper fails because it ignores the point that everyone can be seen as a precursor of everyone else, e.g. Aquinas as a precursor of Popper.

4 Russell tells of his encounter with Lawrence in (1956 p. 107).

5 This is said to allow for recent therapeutic ideas that mental disturbance can be an option that is at some level chosen and which is disentangleable, if at all, only by seeking the hidden goals or pay-offs that make the choice rational, i.e. goal-directed and hence an application of reason to tasks. The hidden character of the goals, and the failure to realize overt goals, precludes learning from experience.

6 'Reason is, and ought only to be, the slave of the passions, and can never pretend to any other office than to serve and obey them', Hume (1738), Book II, Part III, Sect. 3.

7 Without doubt the modern trigger was Evans-Pritchard's path-breaking (1937). The philosopher of science Michael Polanyi was the first to notice it (1958), followed by the Wittgensteinian Winch (1964). The anthologies of Wilson (1970), Horton and Finnegan (1973) and Hollis and Lukes (1982) show that the iceberg has tips.

8 Instructive in this matter is Winch's gloss on prayer in (1964).

9 Here I strongly dissent from Bacon for whom the aim of science is to gain power over nature.

10 Durkheim (1915) makes no bones about this:

> sociology . . . like every positive science . . . has as its object the explanation of some actual reality which is near to us . . . it is an essential postulate of sociology that a human institution cannot rest upon an error and a lie . . . in reality, there are no religions which are false. All are true in their own fashion; all answer . . . to the given conditions of human existence (pp. 2–4). How could a vain fantasy have been able to fashion the human consciousness so strongly and durably? Surely it ought to be a principle of the science of religions that religion expresses nothing which does not exist in nature; for there are sciences only of natural phenomena . . . how has this extraordinary dupery been able to perpetuate itself all through the course of history? (p. 70). The believer is not deceived when he believes in the existence of a moral power upon which he depends and from which he receives all that is best in himself: this power exists, it is society (p. 225).

11 My last publications of the cults were (1970, 1972) and since then a number of useful publications have come to my attention, including Burridge (1969a, 1969b, 1973, 1979), Burton-Bradley (1970, 1973), Christiansen (1969), Lawrence (1971), Lawrence and Meggitt (1965), Machlin (1970), Morauta (1972), Schwartz (1962, 1971, 1976), Ryan (1969), Steinbauer (1978), Valentine (1963), Wallis (1943). On the question of status, Cochrane's (1970) reconsideration of the Vailala Madness and Marching Rule is most instructive. Sociologists are familiar with the idea of cults as status defence, and Cochrane, sharpening up the views of Belshaw, Burridge and myself, argues for reading them as *status assertion*. That is, the power and material goods of the white men signify more for the status they confer than the comforts and convenience they offer. Hence attempts to get these goods are less significant than the parodies of the white man's social organization which are devised. He thinks that the cults stem from the status problems created by white men who manifestly themselves had status, but who carelessly undermined the native status system by not acknowledging the local 'big men' and, in many cases, while they themselves were a new kind of big men, they did not assume the responsibilities of native big men. Where indigenous status was acknowledged cults ceased, where it was not they may have petered out or continued *sub rosa*.

12 Recent work on the Ghost Dance includes Utley (1963), Dobyns and Euler (1967), Dempsey (1968).

13 Worsley retreated somewhat from his Marxist reading in the second edition of 1957 (1968). Gellner's theory of nationalism will not fit Melanesia because he sees common language, culture and literacy as the essential nexus (Gellner 1973b, 1975, 1983).

14 This is a gloss on many of the cults, see Jarvie 1964a, 1970, 1972a, for more detail.

15 Collingwood's theory of presuppositions (1940, pp. 21–77) allows them to become visible only in retrospect and leaves us with the very difficult problem of explaining their change.

134

16 Indeed Stent (1977) has argued that the cult framework of thought is as immovable as a Kuhnian paradigm within which each individual variant cult is 'normal science'.

17 Cochrane (1970) also defends the rationality of the cultists stoutly, but neglects the possibility that rationality is something we can learn to improve: 'The events of 1919 in the Gulf Division, Papua, were neither "extraordinary" nor can they be described as "madness". Nor can the events of 1944 or 1963 be thought of as "irrational". All these events were purposive and logical in the light of indigenous knowledge' (p. 171).

18 Such that an eminent anthropologist in a text-book Gluckman (1965) makes a point of trying to spike such reasoning (pp. 2, 4, 6, 9, 17, 19).

19 Ruth Bunzel, in a non-apologetic Introduction to Lévy-Bruhl (1910) English translation, informs us that he changed his formulation later to logical and mystical forms of thinking, both of them copresent. At xvii she cites a passage from his posthumously published notebooks where he explicitly withdraws the suggestion that pre-logical or mystical mentality is prior.

20 This rule is an equivocation on the word 'contained'. Ordinary usage suggests 'held within'. In logic it means 'validly derivable from'. Hence p v q is 'contained' in p, since $p \supset (p v q)$ is a tautology. This explains why there is more contained in scientific theories than appears in their formulation. See Musgrave (1961).

Part two Relativism

1 'The real difficulty encountered in the understanding of primitive thought is not as some philosophers suppose, that its "supernatural" beliefs are refractory to rational understanding, but that symbolism is linguistically untranslatable and its ideas encapsulated in action, ritual, and social institutions; that is, they exist at a sub-verbal level' (Hallpike 1979, p. 485).

2 Although one could make the argument that, like a protest march, they may dramatize the Melanesians' plight and serve to galvanize the authorities to diagnose what is wrong and do something. That doing something, significantly, will not consist of prayer, religious organization, etc.

3 Herskovits expressed it by asking, rhetorically: 'whose standards' (1958, p. 270), see below.

4 See also Stent (1977, pp. 189–90).

5 I have in mind particularly Moser (1968), Tennekes (1971), Trigg (1973), and my own (1974, 1975, 1976).

6 The following reviews of it are worth noting: *Saturday Review*, 14 October, 1972; *New York Times Book Review*, 12 November, 1972; *New Yorker*, 18 November, 1972.

7 An undirected response is one where the investigator responds to questions and assertions by mirroring them in his own speech, offering neither affirmation nor denial. It is beautifully caricatured

in the Lurie novel *Imaginary Friends*, which I discuss in the Epilogue.

8 On face see Jarvie and Agassi (1970), Ng (1980), Hu (1944) and Stover (1962).

9 See Gier (1980) for a guide to this topic, and note also Agassi (1981).

10 See my discussion of all this in (1972, ch. II); and Bloor (1973, 1976).

11 See his (1956), and Gellner's (1957) and Jarvie (1960).

12 I am thinking principally of his *Principia Ethica* (1903).

Part three Rationality and relativism

1 Winch, for example, in his comments on my (1970) remarks:

> I do, however, want to protest very stongly against the sort of claim that creeps into Jarvie's paper towards the end to the effect that the almost universal success of western ways of life in ousting other 'more primitive' ways shows anything about the superior rationality (or superior anything else, except persuasiveness) of western institutions. In this connection I should like to remind Mr. Jarvie both of Plato's remarks about the difference between persuasion and instruction in his *Gorgias* (as well as what he says about 'The Great Beast' in *The Republic*) and also of Sir Karl Popper's criticisms of moral and other forms of historicism (1970, pp. 258–9).

2 I am referring to a notorious paper by Lewis Carroll in which he showed that someone sceptical of an inference can always demand further premisses and so resist persuasion. A bulky literature developed trying to wriggle out of this. A simple point was overlooked: inferences are arguments and arguments do not force assent, assent is a psychological matter. It took the work of Bartley (1962) to clear the matter up with a non-justificationist reading of logic, and a sharp use of the object-language/meta-language distinction. One's hopes for rational debate, and one's idea that there is some progress in philosophy have to be severely tested by the tendency to overlook this article. Barnes and Bloor (1982) in discussing it and surveying the literature (p. 41) do not even list Bartley's solution.

3 A correction is needed to the idea that assessment is to be relativised to cultures. Influential philosophers have proposed alternatives. Thomas Kuhn (1962) ties the assessment of ideas either to paradigms, when what is going on is normal science, and no assessment at all when extraordinary or revolutionary science is afoot. Stephen Toulmin ties assessment to fields, that is academic or practical subjects and explicitly denies that there are field-independent assessment procedures (Toulmin 1958, 1972, and Jarvie 1976). A figure to whom both are indebted, L. Wittgenstein, ties assessment to forms of life (Wittgenstein 1954, §§ 241, 242, Gier 1980).

4 Indeed, Collingwood thought ultimate presuppositions only became visible to later generations freed from them (Collingwood 1940).
5 However, Martin Hollis has tried vigorously to make the case that even for communication a minimum of presupposition of logic is required (Hollis 1967).
6 In additon to Mannheim's work, see Berger and Luckmann (1966), Remmling (1975), Simonds (1978), and Mannheim (1982). Popper's decisive case against Mannheim (1945) has not been rebutted.
7 Morris Ginsberg is a sadly neglected figure, see his (1956).
8 'Non-terminating' disagreements is a term due to W. T. Jones, See, among other places, his (1980).
9 He calls it 'Protagorean relativism'.

Epilogue

1 Mercene Marcoux, in an unpublished paper.
2 R. G. Collingwood held this view in a most interesting form, see his (1940, chapter V); *An Autobiography*, Oxford 1939, ch. VII.
3 *The Revolution in Anthropology*, London 1964; see also 'On Theories of Fieldwork and the Scientific Character of Social Anthropology', *Philosophy of Science*, vol 34, 1967, pp 223–42; 'The Problem of Ethical Integrity in Participant Observation'. *Current Anthropology*, vol. 10, 1969, pp 505–8; 'On the Objectivity of Anthropology,' in R. J. Seeger and R. S. Cohen, eds, *Philosophical Foundations of Science*, Boston Studies in the Philosophy of Science, vol. XI, Dordecht 1974, pp. 317–24; 'Cultural Relativism Again,' *Philosophy of the Social Sciences*, vol. 5, 1975, pp. 342–53.
4 Here I follow Ernest Gellner's intriguing idea that the centrality of epistemology in western philosophy is explainable. See his *Legitimation of Belief*, London 1975.
5 Cp. Gellner's remarks on Husserl in 'Ethnomethodology: the Rechantment Industry, or the Californian Way of Subjectivity,' *Philosophy of the Social Sciences*, vol. 5, 1975, pp. 446–7.
6 She does not, and her explicit allegiance to the brilliant but irrationalist Michael Polanyi confirms this point. Cf. note 22 below.
7 She does not justify her answer by saying information would otherwise be withheld. Whether *deception* is justified as a means of getting anthropological information is an issue I avoid here.
8 The word 'attitude' should not be taken to mean that science depends upon phsychological variables. 'Attitude' can be cashed out as, 'dispositions to act in certain ways', miniature individual versions of the formal laws, rules, and procedures of the institutions of science. These institutions – schools, departments, laboratories, universities, libraries, journals, seminars, conferences, colloquia, books – indeed the invisible college itself, institutionalize scepticism.
9 I borrow the term from Gellner, see, note 5, above, p. 437.
10 K. R. Popper, 'The Logic of the Social Sciences,' in T. W. Adorno, et al., *The Positivist Dispute in German Sociology*, London 1976,

pp. 87–104, especially the Eighth Thesis, pp. 91*ff.* (The original of this important paper appeared in German in *Kölner Zeitschrift für Soziologie und Sozialpsychologie*, vol 14, 1962, pp. 233–43.)

11 I have never, for example, been invited to join the Association of Social Anthropologists of the British Commonwealth, presumably because their basic qualification is an academic teaching post in social anthropology.

12 In 'The Problem of Ethical Integrity . . .', note 3 above, I suggested that doing anthropology essentially involves exploiting the ambiguities of the stranger-friend role.

12 The sociology of religious movements seems to me to incorporate the sociology of intellectual endeavour as its secularized version. Popper has a fascinating distinction between religious or dogmatic schools and critical schools of thought in *Conjectures and Refutations*, London 1963, chapter 5, especially pp. 149–50.

14 Gellner refers ironically to the theories of cognition by trauma and knowledge by total immersion in his 1973b, p. 126.

15 I recall the deep impression made on me by Fred Hoyle's *The Nature of the Universe*, Oxford 1950, and by the radio debates between Bertrand Russell and Father Copleston, and A. J. Ayer and Father Copleston. Such was the calibre of the education one used to get from that magnificent institution known as the BBC Third Programme.

16 I suppose my views are closest to Richard Robinson's *An Atheist's Values*, Oxford 1964.

17 See E. M. Forster, in *I Believe*, London 1940, pp. 42–50.

18 More puzzling is the social marginality such intellectual distancing induces or reinforces. One can read it two ways: either reflection induces and entails marginality, or, reflection is an effort to overcome marginality and achieve re-integration. The latter I find unconvincing. The open-minded society, the reflective, critical society is one in which the bonds of unreflective community cannot exist. See Walter Kaufmann, *Without Guilt and Justice*, New York 1973.

19 Although Leon Festinger et al. (1956) suggested another scenario.

20 This was quite deliberate, and led me to a fierce defence of Tylor and Frazer and the subsequent controversy. See Horton (1967b)

21 For details see my (1964b).

22 Hence the appositeness of Jules-Rosette's reference to Polanyi, whose philosophy of science strikes me as dogmatic and irrational.

23 A sketch for a reading of the history of anthropology in these terms is my (1972).

24 For further discussion of this problem of how seriously to take religious and anthropological doctrines, see my (1976).

25 Her novels in sequence are: *The Nowhere City*, New York 1965; *Imaginary Friends*, New York 1967; *Real People*. New York 1969; *Love and Friendship*, New York 1972; and *The War Between the Tates*, New York 1975; *Only Children*, New York 1979. Page numbers refer to the Avon paperback edition.

Bibliography

Acosta, Joseph de 1590, *Historia Natural y Moral de las Indias*, Seville
(English translation 1963).

Agassi, Joseph, 1959, 'Epistemology as an Aid to Science', *British
Journal for the Philosophy of Science*, vol. 10, pp. 135–46.

Agassi, Joseph, 1963, *Towards an Historiography of Science, History
and Theory*, Beiheft 2.

Agassi, Joseph, 1964, 'The Nature of Scientific Problems and their
Roots in Metaphysics', in M. Bunge, ed., *The Critical Approach*,
Chicago pp. 189–211.

Agassi, Joseph, 1973, 'Testing as a Bootstrap Operation in Physics',
Zeitschrfit für Allegemeine Wissenschaft, vol. 4, pp. 1–25.

Agassi, Joseph, 1975, *Science in Flux*, Dordrecht.

Agassi, Joseph, 1977, *Towards A Rational Philosophical Anthropology*,
The Hague.

Agassi, Joseph, 1981, 'Was Wittgenstein Really Necessary?', in his
1981a.

Agassi, Joseph, 1981a, *Science and Society*, Dordrecht.

Allen, Don Cameron, 1949, *The Legend of Noah: Renaissance
Rationalism in Art, Science and Letters*, Illinois Studies in Language
and Literature, vol. 33, nos 3–4, Urbana.

Bacon, Sir Francis, 1620, *Novum Organum*, London.

Baldry, H. C., 1965, *The Unity of Mankind in Greek Thought*,
Cambridge.

Barcia Carbillado y Zúniga, Andrés González de, 1729, ed., García
1607, Madrid.

Barnes, Barry and Bloor, David, 1982, 'Relativism, Rationalism and
the Sociology of Knowledge', in Hollis and Lukes, pp. 21–47.

Barth, F., 1974, 'On Responsibility and Humanity: Calling a Colleague
to Account', *Current Anthropology*, vol. 15, pp. 99–103.

Barth, F., 1975, *Ritual and Knowledge Among the Baktaran of New
Guinea*, Oslo.

Bartley, III, W. W., 1962, 'Achilles , the Tortoise and Explanation in

139

Science and History', *British Journal for the Philosophy of Science*, vol. 13, pp. 15–33.

Bartley, III, W. W., 1968, 'Theories of Demarcation Between Science and Metaphysics', in I. Lakatos and A. Musgrave, eds, *Problems in the Philosophy of Science*, Amsterdam, pp. 40–64.

Beattie, J. H. M., 1964, *Other Cultures*, London.

Beattie, J. H. M., 1966, 'Ritual and Social Change', *Man*, vol. 1, pp. 60–74.

Beattie, J. H. M., 1970, 'On Understanding Ritual', in Wilson, ed., pp. 240–68.

Becker, Ernest, 1971, *The Lost Science of Man*, New York.

Belshaw, C. S., 1950, 'The Significance of Modern Cults in Melanesian Development', *Australian Outlook*, vol. 4, pp. 116–25.

Belshaw, C. S., 1954, *Changing Melanesia*, Melbourne.

Berger, Peter and Luckmann, T., 1966, *The Social Construction of Reality*, New York.

Berkhofer Jr., Robert F., 1978, *The White Man's Indian: Images of the American Indian from Columbus to the Present*, New York.

Bloor, David, 1973, 'Wittgenstein and Mannheim on the Sociology of Mathematics', *Studies in the History and Philosophy of Science*, vol. 4, pp. 173–91.

Bloor, David, 1974, 'Popper's Mystification of Objective Knowledge', *Science Studies*, pp. 65–76.

Bloor, David, 1976, *Knowledge and Social Imagery*, London.

Boas, Franz, 1911, *The Mind of Primitive Man*, New York.

Bolt, Christine, 1971, *Victorian Attitudes to Race*, London.

Boon, James A., 1980, 'Comparative De-Enlightenment: Paradox and Limits in the History of Ethnology', *Daedalus*, vol. 109, pp. 73–91.

Briskman, Larry, 1977, 'Historicist Relativism and Bootstrap Rationality', *The Monist*, vol. 60, pp. 509–39.

Burridge, K. O. L., 1960, *Mambu*, London.

Burridge, K. O. L., 1969a, *Tangu Traditions*, Oxford.

Burrridge, K. O. L., 1969b, *New Heaven New Earth*, Oxford.

Burridge, K. O. L., 1973, *Encountering Aborigines*, New York.

Burridge, K. O. L., 1979, *Someone, No One*, Princeton.

Burrow, J. W., 1966, *Evolution and Society*, Cambridge.

Burton-Bradley, B. G., 1970, 'The New Guinea Prophet: Is the Cultist Always Abnormal?' *Med. J. Austr.*, vol. 1, pp. 124–9.

Burton-Bradley, B. G., 1973, 'The Psychiatry of Cargo Cult', *Med J. Austr.*, vol. 2, pp. 388–92.

Burtt, E.A., 1925, *The Metaphysical Foundations of Modern Science*, London.

Bury, J. B., 1932, *The Idea of Progress: An Inquiry into Its Origin and Growth*, New York.

Chagnon, Napoleon, 1968, *The Yanomamo: The Fierce People*, New York.

Chagnon, Napoleon, 1974, *Studying the Yanomamo*, New York.

Christiansen, Palle, 1969, *The Melanesian Cargo Cult, Millenarianism as a Factor in Cultural Change*, Copenhagen.

140

Cochrane, Glynn, 1970, *Big Men and Cargo Cults*, Oxford.

Collingwood, R. G., 1940, *An Essay on Metaphysics*, Oxford.

Coon, Carleton, S., 1962, *The Origin of Races*, New York.

Curtin, Philip D., 1964, *The Image of Africa, British Ideas and Action 1980–1850*, Madison.

De Laguna, Grace, 1942, 'Cultural Relativism and Science', *Philosophical Review*, vol. 51, pp. 141–66.

De Laguna, Grace, 1949, 'Culture and Rationality', *American Anthropologist*, vol. 51, pp. 379–91.

Dempsey, Hugh A., 1968, *Blackfoot Ghost Dance*, Calgary.

Dixon, Keith, 1977, 'Is Cultural Relativism Self-Refuting?', *British Journal of Sociology*, vol. 28, pp. 75–88.

Dobyns, Henry F. and Euler, Robert C., 1967, *The Ghost Dance of 1880 Among the Pai Indians of the Northwestern Arizona*, Prescott College.

Duncker, Karl, 1939, 'Ethical Relativity?', *Mind*, vol. 48, pp. 39–57.

Durkheim, Emile, 1915, *Elementary Forms of the Religious Life*, London.

Eggan, Fred, 1954, 'Social Anthropology and Controlled Comparison', *American Anthropologist*, vol. 56, pp. 743–6.

Eggan, Fred, 1969, '100 Years of Ethnology and Social Anthropology', in J. O. Brew, ed., *One Hundred Years of Anthropology*, Cambridge, Mass.

Eliot, John, 1660, 'The Learned Conjectures of Mr. John Eliot touching the Americans, of New and notable consideration, written to Mr. Thorowgood', in Thorowgood, 1660, pp. 1–28.

Elliott, J. H., 1972, 'The Discovery of America and the Discovery of Man', *Proc. Brit. Academy*, vol. 58, pp. 101–25.

L'Estrange, Hamon, 1662, *Americans no Iewes, or Improbabilities that the Americans are of that Race*, London: W. W. for Henry Seile.

Evans-Pritchard, E. E., 1934, 'Lévy-Bruhl's Theory of Primitive Mentality, reprinted in the *Journal of the Anthropological Society of Oxford*, vol. 1, pp. 39–60.

Evans-Pritchard, E. E., 1937, *Witchcraft, Oracles and Magic Among the Azande*, Oxford.

Evans-Pritchard, E. E., 1950, *Social Anthropology*, London.

Evans-Pritchard, E. E., 1965, *Theories of Primitive Religion*, Oxford.

Evans-Pritchard, E. E., 1981, *A History of Social Anthropology*, London.

Eysenck, H. J., 1981, *The Intelligence Controversy*, New York.

Festinger, Leon, Henry W. Riecken and Stanley Schachter, 1956, *When Prophecy Fails*, New York.

Firth, Raymond, 1951, 'Contemporary British Social Anthropology', *American Anthropologist*, vol. 53, pp. 474–89.

Fortune, Reo, 1932, *Sorcerers of Dobu*, London.

Foster, Robert, 1971, 'The Cargo Cults Today', *New Society*, vol. 17, pp. 10–12.

Frazer, Sir James, 1911–36, *The Golden Bough*, London.

Fredrickson, George M., 1971, *The Black Image in the White Mind*, New York.

Freedman, Maurice, 1978, *Main Trends in Social and Cultural Anthropology*, New York.

García, Gregorio, 1607, *Origen de los Indios de el Nuevo Mundo, e Indias Occidentales*, Valencia.

Gayton, A. H., 1930–31, 'The Ghost Dance of 1879 in South-Central California', *University of California Publications in American Archaeology and Ethnology*, vol. XXVIII, pp. 57–82.

Gellner, E. A., 1957, Review of Morris Ginsberg, *On the Diversity of Morals* and *Reason and Unreason in Society*, *Universities Quarterly*, vol. 12, November, pp. 83–91.

Gellner, E. A., 1959, *Words and Things*, London.

Gellner, E. A., 1964, *Thought and Change*, London.

Gellner, E. A., 1973a, 'Scale and Nation', *Philosophy of the Social Sciences*, vol. 3, pp. 1–17.

Gellner, E.A., 1973b, *Cause and Meaning in the Social Sciences*, London.

Gellner, E.A., 1975, *Legitimation of Belief*, Cambridge.

Gellner, E.A., 1980, *Spectacles and Predicaments*, Cambridge.

Gellner, E.A., 1983, *Nationalism*, Oxford.

Gier, Nicholas F., 1980, 'Wittgenstein and Forms of Life', *Philosophy of the Social Sciences*, vol. 10, pp. 241–58.

Ginsberg, Morris, 1947, *Reason and Unreason in Society*, London.

Ginsberg, Morris, 1956, *On the Diversity of Morals*, London.

Gluckman, Max, 1965, *Politics, Law and Ritual in Tribal Society*, Oxford.

Gombrich, E. H., 1961, *Art and Illusion*, London.

Gossett, Thomas F., 1963, *Race, The History of an Idea in America*, Dallas.

Hallpike, C. R., 1979, *The Foundations of Primitive Thought*, Oxford.

Hanke, Lewis, 1949, *The Spanish Struggle for Justice in the Conquest of America*, Boston.

Hanke, Lewis, 1959, *Aristotle and the American Indians, A Study in Race Prejudice in the Modern World*, Bloomington.

Hanke, Lewis, 1974, *All Mankind is One*, DeKalb.

Hanson, F. Allan, 1975, *Meaning in Culture*, London.

Hanson, F. Allan, 1981, 'Anthropologie und die Rationalitätsdebatte', in H. P. Duerr, ed., *Der Wissenschaft und das Irationale*, Frankfurt, pp. 245–72.

Harding, T. G. and Lawrence, P., 1971, 'Cash Crops or Cargo?', in A. L. Epstein et al. eds, *The Politics of Dependence*, Canberra.

Harris, Marvin, 1968, *The Rise of Anthropological Theory*, New York.

Hatch, Elvin, 1973, *Theories of Man and Culture*, New York.

Hatch Elvin, 1983, *Culture and Morality, The Relativity of Values in Anthropology*, New York.

Hattiangadi, J. N., 1978/9, 'The Structure of Problems, Parts I and II',

Philosophy of the Social Sciences, vol 8, pp. 345–65, vol. 9, pp. 49–76.

Hattangadi, J. N., 1983, 'Three Contemporary Problems of Methodology and a Methodology Without Methodological Rules', in R. S. Cohen and M. W. Wartofsky, eds, *Language, Logic and Method*, Dordrecht, pp. 103–51.

Hattiangadi, J. N. and Ziv, N., 1982. 'Essence versus Evolution in Language', *Word*, pp. 73–98.

Hayek, F. A., 1953, *The Counter-Revolution of Science*, Chicago.

Herskovits, M. J., 1942, 'On the Values in Culture', *Scientific Monthly*, vol 54. pp. 557–60.

Herskovits, M. J., 1951, 'Tender and Tough-Minded Anthropology and the Study of Values in Culture', in Herskovits (1973), pp. 35–48.

Herskovits, M. J., 1958, 'Some Further Comments on Cultural Relativism', *American Anthropologist*, vol. 60, pp. 266–73.

Herskovits, M. J., 1973, *Cultural Relativism*, New York.

Hogbin, H. I., 1958, *Social Change*, London.

Hodgen, Margaret, 1964, *Early Anthropology in the 16th and 17th Centuries*, Philadelphia.

Hollis, Martin, 1967, 'Reason and Ritual', *Philosophy*, vol. 47, pp. 231–47.

Hollis, Martin, and Steven Lukes, eds, 1982, *Rationality and Relativism*, Oxford.

Honigman, John J., 1976, *The Development of Anthropological Ideas*, Homewood (Ill.).

Horton, W. R. G., 1964, 'Ritual Man in Africa', *Africa*, vol. 34, pp. 85–103.

Horton, W. R. G., 1967a, 'African Traditional Thought and Western Science', *Africa*, vol. 37, 50–71, 155–87.

Horton, W. R. G., 1967b, 'Neo-Tylorianism: Sound Sense or Sinister Prejudice?', *Man*, vol. 3, pp. 625–34.

Horton, W. R. G., 1973a, 'Lévy-Bruhl, Durkheim and the Scientific Revolution', in Horton and Finnegan 1973, pp. 249–305.

Horton, W. R. G., 1973b, 'Paradox and Explanation', *Philosophy of the Social Sciences*, vol. 3, pp. 231–56, 289–314.

Horton, W. R. G., 1975, 'On the Rationality of Conversion', *Africa*, vol. 45, pp. 219–35, 375–99.

Horton, W. R. G., 1976a, 'Understanding African Traditional Thought' *Second Order*, vol. 5.

Horton, W. R. G., 1976b, 'Professor Winch on Safari', *European Journal of Sociology*, vol. 17, pp. 157–80

Horton, W. R. G., 1979, 'Material-Object Language and Theoretical Language: Towards a Strawsonian Sociology of Thought', in S. C. Brown, ed., *Philosophical Disputes in the Social Sciences*, Brighton, pp. 197–224.

Horton, W. R. G., 1982, 'Tradition and Modernity Revisited', in Hollis and Lukes 1982, pp. 201–60.

Horton, W. R. G., and Finnegan, Ruth, eds, 1973, *Modes of Thought*, London.

Hu, Hsien-Chin, 1944, 'The Chinese Concepts of "Face" ', *American Anthropologist*, vol. 46, pp. 45–64.

Huddleston, Lee Eldridge, 1967, *Origins of the American Indians, European Concepts, 1492–1729*, Austin.

Hume, David, 1738, *A Treatise of Human Nature*, London.

Hunt, James, 1863, 'On the Negro's Place in Nature' in *Memoirs Read Before the Anthropological Society of London*, London, vol. 1.

Jarvie, I. C., 1960, 'Ginsberg on Ethics', *Enquiry*, vol. 2, June, pp. 19–27

Jarvie, I. C., 1964a, 'Theories of Cargo Cults: A Critical Analysis', *Oceania*, vol. 34, pp. 1–31, 108–36.

Jarvie, I. C., 1964b, *The Revolution in Anthropology*, London.

Jarvie, I. C., 1968, 'On the Explanation of Cargo Cults', *European Journal of Sociology*, vol. 7, pp. 299–312.

Jarvie, I. C., 1970, 'Cargo Cults', in *Man, Myth and Magic*, no. 15, pp. 40–12 (London).

Jarvie, I. C., 1972a, 'Cargo Cults', *Encyclopaedia of Papua and New Guinea*, vol. 1, pp.132–7 (Melbourne).

Jarvie, I. C., 1972b, *The Story of Social Anthropology*, New York.

Jarvie, I. C., 1974, 'On the Objectivity of Anthropology', in R. J. Seeger and R. S. Cohen, ed., *Philosophical Foundations of Science*, Dordrecht, pp. 317–24.

Jarvie, I. C., 1975a, 'Cultural Relativism Again', *Philosophy of the Social Sciences*, vol. 5, pp. 343–53.

Jarvie, I. C., 1975b, 'Epistle to the Anthropologists', *American Anthropologist*, vol. 77, pp. 253–66.

Jarvie, I. C., 1976a, 'Nationalism and the Social Sciences', *Canadian Journal of Sociology*, vol. 1, pp. 515–28.

Jarvie, I. C., 1976b, 'Toulmin on the Rationality of Science', in R. S. Cohen, M. W. Wartosfsky and P. K . Feyerabend, eds, *Essays in Memory of Imre Lakatos*, Dordrecht, pp. 311–33.

Jarvie, I. C., 1976c, 'On the Limits of Symbolic Interpretation in Anthropology', *Current Anthropology*, vol. 17, pp. 687–91, 700–1.

Jarvie, I. C., 1979, 'Laudan's Problematic Progress and the Social Sciences', *Philosophy of the Social Sciences*, vol. 9, pp. 484–97.

Jarvie, I. C., 1981, 'Die Anthropologen und das Irrationale' in H. P. Duerr, ed., *Der Wissenschaftler und Das Irrationale*, Frankfurt, pp. 213–44.

Jarvie, I. C. and J. Agassi, 1967, 'The Problem of the Rationality of Magic', *British Journal of Sociology*, vol. 18, pp. 55–74.

Jarvie, I. C. and J. Agassi, 1970, 'A Study in Westernization', in Jarvie and Agassi, eds, *Hong Kong: A Society in Transition*, London, pp. 129–63.

Jarvie, I. C. and J. Agassi, 1973, 'Magic and Rationality Again', *British Journal of Sociology*, vol. 24, pp. 236–45.

Jensen, Arthur R., *Bias in Mental Testing*, London.

Jones, W. T., 1980, 'Reason, Feeling and World View' in P. A. Schilpp, ed., *The Philosophy of Brand Blanshard*, La Salle, Ill., pp. 320–40.

Jordan, Winthrop, 1968, *White over Black*, Chapel Hill.

Jules-Rosette, Bernadetta, 1976, 'The Conversion Experience', *Journal of Religion in Africa*, vol. 7, pp. 132–64.

Jules-Rosette, Bernadetta, 1978, 'The Veil of Objectivity: Prophecy, Divination and Social Inquiry', *American Anthropologist*, vol. 80, pp. 549–70.

Kluckhohn, Clyde K., 1956, 'Towards a Comparison of Value-Emphases in Different Cultures', in Leonard D. White, ed., *The State of the Social Sciences*, Chicago, pp. 116–32.

Kuhn, T. S., 1962, *The Structure of Scientific Revolutions*, Chicago.

Kuper, Adam, 1973, *Anthropologists and Anthropology. The British School 1922–72*, London.

La Péyrère, Isaac de, 1655, *Men Before Adam*, London.

La Péyrère, Isaac de, 1656, *A Theological System Upon That Presupposition, That Men Were Before Adam*, London.

Langham, Ian, 1981, *The Building of British Social Anthropology*, Dordrecht.

Lawrence, Peter, 1954, 'Cargo Cult and Religious Beliefs Among the Garia', *International Archives of Ethnography*, vol. 47 pp. 1–20.

Lawrence, Peter, 1964, *Road Belong Cargo*, Manchester.

Lawrence, Peter, 1971, 'Statements About Religion: The Problem of Rationality', in L. R. Hiatt and C. Jayawardena, eds, *Anthropology in Oceania, Essays Presented to Ian Hogbin*, Sydney, pp. 139–54.

Lawrence, Peter, and Meggitt, M. J., eds, 1965, *Gods, Ghosts and Men in Melanesia*, Melbourne.

Leaf, Murray J., 1979, *Man, Mind and Science*, New York.

Lévy-Bruhl, Lucien, 1910, *Les Fonctions mentales dans les societés inférieurs*, Paris.

Lévy-Bruhl, Lucien, 1922, *La Mentalité primitive*, Paris.

Linton, Ralph, 1952, 'Universal Ethical Principles: An Anthropological View', in Ruth Nanda Anshen, ed., *Moral Principles in Action*, NY.

Linton, Ralph, 1954, 'The Problem of Universal Values', in R. F. Spencer, ed., *Method and Perspective in Anthropology, Papers in honor of Wilson D. Wallis*, Minneapolis, Reprinted 1969, Gloucester, Mass., pp. 145–68.

Lipset, S. M., 1963, *The First New Nation*, New York.

Llobera, J. R., 1976, 'The History of Anthropology as a Problem', *Critique of Anthropology*, no 7, pp. 17–42.

Lloyd, G. E. R., 1979, *Magic, Reason and Experience*, Cambridge.

Lovejoy, A. O., 1936, *The Great Chain of Being*, Cambridge, Mass.

Lovejoy, A. O., and Boas, George, 1935, *Primitivism and Related Ideas in Antiquity*, New York, reprint 1965.

Lowie, R. H., 1937, *A History of Ethnological Theory*, New York.

Maalefit, Annemarie de Waal, 1974, *Images of Man, A History of Anthropological Thought*, New York.

Machlin, Milt, 1970, 'The Tribe that Tried to Buy President Johnson', *Argosy*, vol. 370, no. 6, June, pp. 23–9, 66–8.

Mannheim, Karl, 1982, *Structures of Thinking*, edited by Kettle, Meja, Stehr, London.

Mead, Margaret, 1974, *Ruth Benedict*, New York.

Midgley, Mary, 1978, 'More About Reason, Commitment and Social Anthropology', *Philosophy*, vol. 53, July, pp. 401–3.

Mill, John Stuart, 1859, *On Liberty*, Bantam Matrix Edition of the Essential Works of J. S. Mill, ed., Max Lerner, New York 1961.

Moore, G. E., 1903, *Principia Ethica*, Cambridge.

Morauta, Louise, 1972, 'The Politics of Cargo Cults in the Madang Area', *Man*, vol. 7, pp. 430–47.

Moser, Shia, 1968, *Absolutism and Relativism in Ethics*, Springfield, Ill.

Mounce, H. O., 1973, 'Understanding a Primitive Society', *Philosophy*, vol. 48, pp. 347–62.

Murdock, G. P., 1951, 'British Social Anthropology', *American Anthropologist*, vol 53 pp. 465–73.

Musgrave, Alan, 1961, 'Impersonal Knowledge, A Critique of Subjectivism in Epistemology', PhD thesis, University of London, unpublished.

Ng, Margaret, 1980, 'Is Face the Same as Li? A Critical Note on Jarvie and Agassi "A Study in Westernization" ', *Journal of the Hong Kong Branch of The Royal Asiatic Society*, vol. 18, pp. 49–58.

Nott, J. C. and Gliddon, G. R., 1854, *Types of Mankind or Ethnological Researches*, Philadelphia.

O'Gorman, Edmundo, 1961, *The Invention of America*, Bloomington.

Odom, H. H., 1967, 'Generalizations on Race in Nineteenth Century Physical Anthropology', *Isis*, vol. 58, pp. 5–18.

Pagden, Anthony, 1982, *The Fall of Natural Man: The American-Indian and the Origins of Comparative Ethnology*, Cambridge.

Pearce, Roy H., 1953, *The Savages of America: A Study of the Indian and the Idea of Civilization*, Baltimore,

Polanyi, Michael, 1958, *Personal Knowledge*, London.

Popkin, Richard, 1974a, 'Bible Criticism and Social Science', in *Methodological and Historical Essays in Natural and Social Sciences*, ed., R. S. Cohen and M. W. Wartofsky, Dordrecht, pp. 339–60.

Popkin, Richard, 1974b, 'The Philosophical Bases of Modern Racism', in Craig Walton and John P. Anton, eds, *Philosophy and the Civilising Arts*, Athens, Ohio, pp. 126–65.

Popkin, Richard, 1978, 'Pre Adamism in Nineteenth Century American Thought: "Speculative Biology" and Racism', *Philosophia*, vol. 8, pp. 205–39.

Popper, K. R., 1945, *The Open Society and Its Enemies*, London.

Popper, K. R., 1959, *Logic of Scientific Discovery*, London.

Popper, K. R., 1974, 'Intellectual Autobiography', in P. A. Schilpp, ed., *The Philosophy of Karl Popper*, La Salle, Ill. pp. 3–182.

Popper, K. R., 1983, *Realism and the Aim of Science*, Totowa, N.J.

Radcliffe-Brown, A. R., 1952, *Structure and Function in Primitive Society*, London.

Remmling, Gunter, W., 1975, *The Sociology of Karl Mannheim*, London.

Rice, Edward, 1974, *John Frum He Come*, New York.

Russell, Bertrand, 1912, *The Problems of Philosophy*, Oxford.

Russell, Bertrand, 1956, *Portraits from Memory*, London.

Ryan, D., 1969, 'Christianity, Cargo Cults and Politics Among the Toaripi of Papua', *Oceania*, vol. 41, pp. 99–118.

Sanders, Ronald, 1978, *Lost Tribes and Promised Lands*, Boston.

Schmidt, Paul, F., 1955, 'Some Criticisms of Cultural Relativism', *Journal of Philosophy*, vol. 52, pp. 780–91.

Schwartz, Theodore, 1962, 'The Paliau Movement in the Admiralty Islands, 1946–54', *Anthropological Papers of the American Museum of Natural History*, vol. 49, no. 2.

Schwartz, Theodore, 1971, 'Cargo Cult Frenzy in the South Seas', *Psychology Today*, March, pp. 51–4, 102–3.

Schwartz, Theodore, 1976, 'Cargo Cult: A Melanesian Type-Response to Culture Contact', in G. de Vos, ed., *Responses to Change*, New York, pp. 157–206.

Scholte, Bob, 1978, 'On the Ethnocentricity of Scientistic Logic', *Dialectial Anthropology*, vol. 3, pp. 177–89.

Sheehan, Bernard W., 1980, *Savagism and Civility, Indian and Englishmen in Colonial Virginia*, New York.

Simonds, A. P., 1978, *Karl Mannheim's Sociology of Misunderstanding*, London.

Sinclair, Andrew, 1977, *The Savage: A History of Misunderstanding*, London.

Social Research, 1978, vol. 46, no. 1, Guest Editor, Johannes Fabian, papers by J. F., James Fernandez, Paul S. Breidenbach, William J. Samarin, John M. Janzen, Roy Wagner.

Stanton, William, 1960, *The Leopard's Spots*, Chicago.

Steinbauer, Friedrich, 1978, *Melanesian Cargo Cults: New Salvation Movements in the South Pacific*, St Lucia, Queensland.

Stent, W. R., 1977, 'An Interpretation of a Cargo Cult', *Oceania*, vol. 47, pp. 187–219.

Stepan, Nancy, 1982, *The Idea of Race in Science: Great Britain 1800–1960*, London.

Stocking, George, 1968, *Race, Culture and Evolution*, New York.

Stocking, George, 1971, 'What's in a Name? The Origins of the Royal Anthropological Institute (1837–71)', *Man*, vol. 9, pp. 369–90.

Stoddard, Lothrop, 1920, *The Rising Tide of Color, Against White World-Supremacy*, London.

Stoddard, Lothrop, 1923, *The Revolt Against Civilization, The Menace of the Underman*, New York.

Stoddard, Lothrop, 1924, *Racial Realities in Europe*, New York.

Stoddard, Lothrop, 1926, *Scientific Humanism*, New York.

Stoddard, Lothrop, 1927, *Re-Forging America*, New York.

Stoddard, Lothrop, 1935, *Clashing Tides of Colour*, New York.

Stoddard, Lothrop, 1940, *Into the Darkness*, New York.

Stover, Leon, 1962, ' "Face": Secondary verbal Analogues of Interaction in Chinese Culture', PhD thesis, Columbia University, unpublished.

Tax, Sol, 1955, 'From Lafitau to Radcliffe-Brown. A short History of

147

the Study of Social Organisation', in Fred Eggan, ed., *Social Anthropology of North American Tribes*, Chicago.

Taylor, William Cooke, 1840, *The Natural History of Society, in the Barbarian and Civilised State: An Essay Towards Discovering the Origin and Course of Human Improvement*, London.

Tennekes, J., 1971, *Anthropology, Relativism and Method*, Assen.

Thorowgood, Thomas, 1650, *Iewes in America or Probablities that the Americans are of that Race. With the Removall of some contrary reasoning, and earnest desire for effectual endeavours to make them Christian*, London.

Thorowgood, Thomas, 1660, *Jews in America, or, Probabilities those Indians are Judaical made more probable by some Additionals to the former conjectures*, London.

Toulmin, Stephen, 1958, *The Uses of Argument*, Cambridge.

Toulmin, Stephen, 1972, *Human Understanding*, Princeton.

Trigg, Roger, 1973, *Reason and Commitment*, Cambridge.

Turnbull, Colin, 1972, *The Mountain People*, New York.

Turnbull, Colin, 1974, 'Reply', *Current Anthropology*, vol. 15, p. 103.

Turnbull, Colin, 1975, 'Reply', *Current Anthropology*, vol. 16, pp. 354–8.

Urbach, Peter, 1974, 'Progress and Degeneration in the "I.Q. Debate" ', *British Journal for the Philosophy of Science*, vol. 25, pp. 99–135, 235–59.

Urbach, Peter, 1982, 'Francis Bacon as a Precursor to Popper', *British Journal for the Philosophy of Science*, vol. 33, pp. 113–32.

Utley, Robert, M., 1963, *The Last Days of the Sioux Nation*, New Haven.

Valentine, C., 1963, 'Social Status, Political Power and Native Responses to European Influence in Oceania', *Anthropological Forum*, vol. 1, July, pp. 3–55.

Wallis, Wilson D., 1943, *Messiahs: Their Role in Civilization*, Washington.

Watkins, J. W. N., 1957, 'Between Analytic and Empirical', *Philosophy*, vol. 32, pp. 112–31.

Watkins, J. W. N., 1958, 'Confirmable and Influential Metaphysics', *Mind*, vol. 67, pp. 344–65.

Watkins, J. W. N., 1960, 'When Are Statements Empirical?', *British Journal for the Philosophy of Science*, vol. X, pp. 287–308.

Wellman, Carl, 1963, 'The Ethical Implications of Cultural Relativism', *Journal of Philosophy*, vol. 60, pp. 169–84.

White, A. D., 1896, *A History of the Warfare of Science with Theology*, New York.

White, Leslie, 1966, 'The Social Organisation of Ethnological Theory', *Rice University Studies*, vol. 52, 3–28.

Williams, F. E., 1923, *The Vailala Madness*, Port Moresby.

Wilson, Bryan, ed., 1970, *Rationality*, Oxford.

Winch, Peter, 1958, *The Idea of a Social Science*, London.

Winch, Peter, 1964, 'Understanding a Primitive Society', *American Philosophical Quarterly*, vol. 1, pp. 307–24.

Winch, Peter, 1970, 'Comment', in Robert Borger and Frank Cioffi, eds, *Explanation in the Behavioural Sciences*, Cambridge.

Winchell, Alexander, 1880, *Preadamites; Or a Demonstration of the Existence of Men before Adam*, Chicago.

Wisdom, J. O., 1953, *The Unconscious Origin of Berkeley's Philosophy*, London.

Wisdom. J. O., 1973, 'The Phenomenological Approach to the Sociology of Knowledge', *Philosophy of the Social Sciences*, vol 3, pp. 257–66.

Wittgenstein, L., 1954, *Philosophical Investigations*, Oxford.

Worsley, Peter, 1957, *The Trumpet Shall Sound*, London, Second edition, 1968.

149

Index of names

Index of subjects

t indicates that a term is defined

unintended consequences, 12
United States of America, 16, 111;
  discovery of, 11
unity of mankind, 3–4, 7, 9, 11, 16,
  17, 22, 24, 42, 43, 50, 59, 63, 108;
  as programme, 14–15

Vailala Madness, The, 44
Valladolid, 41

war, 10
what is, is right, 82
When Prophecy Fails, 128
witchcraft, 62, 102, 105
*Witchcraft, Oracles and Magic Among
  the Azande*, 31

Yanomamo, The Fierce People, 77

Routledge Social Science Series

Routledge & Kegan Paul
London, Boston, Melbourne and Henley

39 Store Street, London WC1E 7DD
9 Park Street, Boston, Mass 02108
296 Beaconsfield Parade, Middle Park,
Melbourne, 3206 Australia
Broadway House, Newtown Road,
Henley-on-Thames, Oxon RG9 1EN

Contents

*Authors wishing to submit manuscripts for any series
in this catalogue should send them to the Social Science Editor,
Routledge & Kegan Paul plc, 39 Store Street,
London WC1E 7DD.*
● *Books so marked are available in paperback also.*
○ *Books so marked are available in paperback only.*
*All books are in metric Demy 8vo format (216 × 138mm approx.)
unless otherwise stated.*

International Library of Sociology
General Editor John Rex

GENERAL SOCIOLOGY

Alexander, J. Theoretical Logic in Sociology.
 Volume 1: Positivism, Presuppositions and Current Controversies. *234 pp.*
 Volume 2: The Antinomies of Classical Thought: *Marx and Durkheim.*
 Volume 3: The Classical Attempt at Theoretical Synthesis: *Max Weber.*
 Volume 4: The Modern Reconstruction of Classical Thought: *Talcott Parsons.*
Barnsley, J. H. The Social Reality of Ethics. *464 pp.*
Brown, Robert. Explanation in Social Science. *208 pp.*
● Rules and Laws in Sociology. *192 pp.*
Bruford, W. H. Chekhov and His Russia. *A Sociological Study. 244 pp.*
Burton, F. and **Carlen, P.** Official Discourse. *On Discourse Analysis, Government Publications, Ideology. 160 pp.*
Cain, Maureen E. Society and the Policeman's Role. *326 pp.*
● **Fletcher, Colin.** Beneath the Surface. *An Account of Three Styles of Sociological Research. 221 pp.*
Gibson, Quentin. The Logic of Social Enquiry. *240 pp.*
Glassner, B. Essential Interactionism. *208 pp.*
Glucksmann, M. Structuralist Analysis in Contemporary Social Thought. *212 pp.*
Gurvitch, Georges. Sociology of Law. *Foreword by Roscoe Pound. 264 pp.*
Hinkle, R. Founding Theory of American Sociology 1881–1913. *376 pp.*
Homans, George C. Sentiments and Activities. *336 pp.*
Johnson, Harry M. Sociology: *A Systematic Introduction. Foreword by Robert K. Merton. 710 pp.*
● **Keat, Russell** and **Urry, John.** Social Theory as Science. *Second Edition. 278 pp.*
Mannheim, Karl. Essays on Sociology and Social Psychology. *Edited by Paul Keckskemeti. With Editorial Note by Adolph Lowe. 344 pp.*
Martindale, Don. The Nature and Types of Sociological Theory. *292 pp.*
● **Maus, Heinz.** A Short History of Sociology. *234 pp.*
Merquior, J. G. Rousseau and Weber. *A Study in the Theory of Legitimacy. 240 pp.*
Myrdal, Gunnar. Value in Social Theory: *A Collection of Essays on Methodology. Edited by Paul Streeten. 332 pp.*
Ogburn, William F. and **Nimkoff, Meyer F.** A Handbook of Sociology. *Preface by Karl Mannheim. 656 pp. 46 figures. 35 tables.*
Parsons, Talcott and **Smelser, Neil J.** Economy and Society: *A Study in the Integration of Economic and Social Theory. 362 pp.*
Payne, G., Dingwall, R., Payne, J. and **Carter, M.** Sociology and Social Research. *336 pp.*
Podgórecki, A. Practical Social Sciences. *144 pp.*
Podgórecki, A. and **Łos, M.** Multidimensional Sociology. *268 pp.*
Raffel, S. Matters of Fact. *A Sociological Inquiry. 152 pp.*
● **Rex, John.** Key Problems of Sociological Theory. *220 pp.*
 Sociology and the Demystification of the Modern World. *282 pp.*
● **Rex, John.** (Ed.) Approaches to Sociology. *Contributions by Peter Abell, Frank Bechhofer, Basil Bernstein, Ronald Fletcher, David Frisby, Miriam Glucksmann, Peter Lassman, Herminio Martins, John Rex, Roland Robertson, John Westergaard and Jock Young. 302 pp.*
Rigby, A. Alternative Realities. *352 pp.*
Roche, M. Phenomenology, Language and the Social Sciences. *374 pp.*
Sahay, A. Sociological Analysis. *220 pp.*
Strasser, Hermann. The Normative Structure of Sociology. *Conservative and Emancipatory Themes in Social Thought. 286 pp.*

Strong, P. Ceremonial Order of the Clinic. *267 pp.*
Urry, J. Reference Groups and the Theory of Revolution. *244 pp.*
Weinberg, E. Development of Sociology in the Soviet Union. *173 pp.*

FOREIGN CLASSICS OF SOCIOLOGY

● **Gerth, H. H.** and **Mills, C. Wright.** From Max Weber: *Essays in Sociology. 502 pp.*
● **Tönnies, Ferdinand.** Community and Association (*Gemeinschaft und Gesell-schaft*). *Translated and Supplemented by Charles P. Loomis. Foreword by Pitirim A. Sorokin. 334 pp.*

SOCIAL STRUCTURE

Andreski, Stanislav. Military Organization and Society. *Foreword by Professor A. R. Radcliffe-Brown. 226 pp. 1 folder.*
Bozzoli, B. The Political Nature of a Ruling Class. *Capital and Ideology in South Africa 1890–1939. 396 pp.*
Bauman, Z. Memories of Class. *The Prehistory and After life of Class. 240 pp.*
Broom, L., Lancaster Jones, F., McDonnell, P. and **Williams, T.** The Inheritance of Inequality. *208 pp.*
Carlton, Eric. Ideology and Social Order. *Foreword by Professor Philip Abrahams. 326 pp.*
Clegg, S. and **Dunkerley, D.** Organization, Class and Control. *614 pp.*
Coontz, Sydney H. Population Theories and the Economic Interpretation. *202 pp.*
Coser, Lewis. The Functions of Social Conflict. *204 pp.*
Crook, I. and **D.** The First Years of the Yangyi Commune. *304 pp., illustrated.*
Dickie-Clark, H. F. Marginal Situation: *A Sociological Study of a Coloured Group. 240 pp. 11 tables.*
Fidler, J. The British Business Elite. *Its Attitudes to Class, Status and Power. 332 pp.*
Giner, S. and **Archer, M. S.** (Eds) Contemporary Europe: *Social Structures and Cultural Patterns. 336 pp.*
● **Glaser, Barney** and **Strauss, Anselm L.** Status Passage: *A Formal Theory. 212 pp.*
Glass, D. V. (Ed.) Social Mobility in Britain. *Contributions by J. Berent, T. Bottomore, R. C. Chambers, J. Floud, D. V. Glass, J. R. Hall, H. T. Himmelweit, R. K. Kelsall, F. M. Martin, C. A. Moser, R. Mukherjee and W. Ziegel. 420 pp.*
Kelsall, R. K. Higher Civil Servants in Britain: *From 1870 to the Present Day. 268 pp. 31 tables.*
● **Lawton, Denis.** Social Class, Language and Education. *192 pp.*
McLeish, John. The Theory of Social Change. *Four Views Considered. 128 pp.*
● **Marsh, David C.** The Changing Social Structure of England and Wales, 1871–1961. *Revised edition. 288 pp.*
Menzies, Ken. Talcott Parsons and the Social Image of Man. *206 pp.*
● **Mouzelis, Nicos.** Organization and Bureaucracy. *An Analysis of Modern Theories. 240 pp.*
● **Ossowski, Stanislaw.** Class Structure in the Social Consciousness. *210 pp.*
● **Podgórecki, Adam.** Law and Society. *302 pp.*
Ratcliffe, P. Racism and Reaction. *A Profile of Handsworth. 388 pp.*
Renner, Karl. Institutions of Private Law and Their Social Functions. *Edited, with an Introduction and Notes, by O. Kahn-Freud. Translated by Agnes Schwarzschild. 316 pp.*
Rex, J. and **Tomlinson, S.** Colonial Immigrants in a British City. *A Class Analysis. 368 pp.*
Smooha, S. Israel. *Pluralism and Conflict. 472 pp.*
Strasser, H. and **Randall, S. C.** An Introduction to Theories of Social Change. *300 pp.*

Wesolowski, W. Class, Strata and Power. *Trans. and with Introduction by G. Kolankiewicz. 160 pp.*

Zureik, E. Palestinians in Israel. *A Study in Internal Colonialism. 264 pp.*

SOCIOLOGY AND POLITICS

Acton, T. A. Gypsy Politics and Social Change. *316 pp.*

Burton, F. Politics of Legitimacy. *Struggles in a Belfast Community. 250 pp.*

Crook, I. and **D.** Revolution in a Chinese Village. *Ten Mile Inn. 216 pp., illustrated.*

de Silva, S. B. D. The Political Economy of Underdevelopment. *640 pp.*

Etzioni-Halevy, E. Political Manipulation and Administrative Power. *A Comparative Study. 228 pp.*

Fielding, N. The National Front. *260 pp.*

● **Hechter, Michael.** Internal Colonialism. *The Celtic Fringe in British National Development, 1536–1966. 380 pp.*

Levy, N. The Foundations of the South African Cheap Labour System. *367 pp.*

Kornhauser, William. The Politics of Mass Society. *272 pp. 20 tables.*

● **Korpi, W.** The Working Class in Welfare Capitalism. *Work, Unions and Politics in Sweden. 472 pp.*

Kroes, R. Soldiers and Students. *A Study of Right- and Left-wing Students. 174 pp.*

Martin, Roderick. Sociology of Power. *214 pp.*

Merquior, J. G. Rousseau and Weber. *A Study in the Theory of Legitimacy. 286 pp.*

Myrdal, Gunnar. The Political Element in the Development of Economic Theory. *Translated from the German by Paul Streeten. 282 pp.*

Preston, P. W. Theories of Development. *296 pp.*

Varma, B. N. The Sociology and Politics of Development. *A Theoretical Study. 236 pp.*

Wong, S.-L. Sociology and Socialism in Contemporary China. *160 pp.*

Wootton, Graham. Workers, Unions and the State. *188 pp.*

CRIMINOLOGY

Ancel, Marc. Social Defence: *A Modern Approach to Criminal Problems. Foreword by Leon Radzinowicz. 240 pp.*

Athens, L. Violent Criminal Acts and Actors. *104 pp.*

Cain, Maureen E. Society and the Policeman's Role. *326 pp.*

Cloward, Richard A. and **Ohlin, Lloyd E.** Delinquency and Opportunity: *A Theory of Delinquent Gangs. 248 pp.*

Downes, David M. The Delinquent Solution. *A Study in Subcultural Theory. 296 pp.*

Friedlander, Kate. The Psycho-Analytical Approach to Juvenile Delinquency: *Theory, Case Studies, Treatment. 320 pp.*

Gleuck, Sheldon and **Eleanor.** Family Environment and Delinquency. *With the statistical assistance of Rose W. Kneznek. 340 pp.*

Lopez-Rey, Manuel. Crime. *An Analytical Appraisal. 288 pp.*

Mannheim, Hermann. Comparative Criminology: *A Text Book. Two volumes. 442 pp. and 380 pp.*

Morris, Terence. The Criminal Area: *A Study in Social Ecology. Foreword by Hermann Mannheim. 232 pp. 25 tables. 4 maps.*

Rock, Paul. Making People Pay. *338 pp.*

● **Taylor, Ian, Walton, Paul** and **Young, Jock.** The New Criminology. *For a Social Theory of Deviance. 325 pp.*

● **Taylor, Ian, Walton, Paul** and **Young, Jock.** (Eds) Critical Criminology. *268 pp.*

SOCIAL PSYCHOLOGY

Bagley, Christopher. The Social Psychology of the Epileptic Child. *320 pp.*
Brittan, Arthur. Meanings and Situations. *224 pp.*
Carroll, J. Break-Out from the Crystal Palace. *200 pp.*
● **Fleming, C. M.** Adolescence: Its Social Psychology. *With an Introduction to recent findings from the fields of Anthropology, Physiology, Medicine, Psychometrics and Sociometry. 288 pp.*
● The Social Psychology of Education: *An Introduction and Guide to Its Study. 136 pp.*
Linton, Ralph. The Cultural Background of Personality. *132 pp.*
● **Mayo, Elton.** The Social Problems of an Industrial Civilization. *With an Appendix on the Political Problem. 180 pp.*
Ottaway, A. K. C. Learning Through Group Experience. *176 pp.*
Plummer, Ken. Sexual Stigma. *An Interactionist Account. 254 pp.*
● **Rose, Arnold M.** (Ed.) Human Behaviour and Social Processes: *an Interactionist Approach. Contributions by Arnold M. Rose, Ralph H. Turner, Anselm Strauss, Everett C. Hughes, E. Franklin Frazier, Howard S. Becker et al. 696 pp.*
Smelser, Neil J. Theory of Collective Behaviour. *448 pp.*
Stephenson, Geoffrey M. The Development of Conscience. *128 pp.*
Young, Kimball. Handbook of Social Psychology. *658 pp. 16 figures. 10 tables.*

SOCIOLOGY OF THE FAMILY

Bell, Colin R. Middle Class Families: *Social and Geographical Mobility. 224 pp.*
Burton, Lindy. Vulnerable Children. *272 pp.*
Gavron, Hannah. The Captive Wife: *Conflicts of Household Mothers. 190 pp.*
George, Victor and **Wilding, Paul.** Motherless Families. *248 pp.*
Klein, Josephine. Samples from English Cultures.
    1. Three Preliminary Studies and Aspects of Adult Life in England. *447 pp.*
    2. Child-Rearing Practices and Index. *247 pp.*
Klein, Viola. The Feminine Character. *History of an Ideology. 244 pp.*
McWhinnie, Alexina M. Adopted Children. *How They Grow Up. 304 pp.*
● **Morgan, D. H. J.** Social Theory and the Family. *188 pp.*
● **Myrdal, Alva** and **Klein, Viola.** Women's Two Roles: *Home and Work. 238 pp. 27 tables.*
Parsons, Talcott and **Bales, Robert F.** Family: Socialization and Interaction Process. *In collaboration with James Olds, Morris Zelditch and Philip E. Slater. 456 pp. 50 figures and tables.*

SOCIAL SERVICES

Bastide, Roger. The Sociology of Mental Disorder. *Translated from the French by Jean McNeil. 260 pp.*
Carlebach, Julius. Caring for Children in Trouble. *266 pp.*
George, Victor. Foster Care. *Theory and Practice. 234 pp.*
    Social Security: *Beveridge and After. 258 pp.*
George, V. and **Wilding, P.** Motherless Families. *248 pp.*
● **Goetschius, George W.** Working with Community Groups. *256 pp.*
Goetschius, George W. and **Tash, Joan.** Working with Unattached Youth. *416 pp.*
Heywood, Jean S. Children in Care. *The Development of the Service for the Deprived Child. Third revised edition. 284 pp.*
King, Roy D., Raynes, Norma V. and **Tizard, Jack.** Patterns of Residential Care. *356 pp.*
Leigh, John. Young People and Leisure. *256 pp.*
● **Mays, John.** (Ed.) Penelope Hall's Social Services of England and Wales. *368 pp.*

Morris Mary. Voluntary Work and the Welfare State. *300 pp.*
Nokes. P. L. The Professional Task in Welfare Practice. *152 pp.*
Timms, Noel. Psychiatric Social Work in Great Britain (1939–1962). *280 pp.*
● Social Casework: *Principles and Practice. 256 pp.*

SOCIOLOGY OF EDUCATION

Banks, Olive. Parity and Prestige in English Secondary Education: a Study in Educational Sociology. *272 pp.*
● **Blyth, W. A. L.** English Primary Education. *A Sociological Description.* 2. Background. *168 pp.*
Collier, K. G. The Social Purposes of Education: *Personal and Social Values in Education. 268 pp.*
Evans, K. M. Sociometry and Education. *158 pp.*
● **Ford, Julienne.** Social Class and the Comprehensive School. *192 pp.*
Foster, P. J. Education and Social Change in Ghana. *336 pp. 3 maps.*
Fraser, W. R. Education and Society in Modern France. *150 pp.*
Grace, Gerald R. Role Conflict and the Teacher. *150 pp.*
Hans, Nicholas. New Trends in Education in the Eighteenth Century. *278 pp. 19 tables.*
● Comparative Education: *A Study of Educational Factors and Traditions. 360 pp.*
● **Hargreaves, David.** Interpersonal Relations and Education. *432 pp.*
● Social Relations in a Secondary School. *240 pp.*
School Organization and Pupil Involvement. *A Study of Secondary Schools.*
● **Mannheim, Karl** and **Stewart, W. A. C.** An Introduction to the Sociology of Education. *206 pp.*
● **Musgrove, F.** Youth and the Social Order. *176 pp.*
● **Ottaway, A. K. C.** Education and Society: An Introduction to the Sociology of Education. *With an Introduction by W. O. Lester Smith. 212 pp.*
Peers, Robert. Adult Education: *A Comparative Study. Revised edition. 398 pp.*
Stratta, Erica. The Education of Borstal Boys. *A Study of their Educational Experiences prior to, and during, Borstal Training. 256 pp.*
● **Taylor, P. H., Reid, W. A.** and **Holley, B. J.** The English Sixth Form. *A Case Study in Curriculum Research. 198 pp.*

SOCIOLOGY OF CULTURE

● **Eppel, E. M.** and **M.** Adolescents and Morality: *A Study of some Moral Values and Dilemmas of Working Adolescents in the Context of a changing Climate of Opinion. Foreword by W. J. H. Sprott. 268 pp. 39 tables.*
● **Fromm, Erich.** The Fear of Freedom. *286 pp.*
● The Sane Society. *400 pp.*
Johnson, L. The Cultural Critics. *From Matthew Arnold to Raymond Williams. 233 pp.*
Mannheim, Karl. Essays on the Sociology of Culture. *Edited by Ernst Mannheim in co-operation with Paul Kecskemeti. Editorial Note by Adolph Lowe. 280 pp.*
Structures of Thinking. *Edited by David Kettler, Volker Meja and Nico Stehr. 304 pp.*
Merquior, J. G. The Veil and the Mask. *Essays on Culture and Ideology. Foreword by Ernest Gellner. 140 pp.*
Zijderfeld, A. C. On Clichés. *The Supersedure of Meaning by Function in Modernity. 150 pp.*
Reality in a Looking Glass. *Rationality through an Analysis of Traditional Folly. 208 pp.*

SOCIOLOGY OF RELIGION

Argyle, Michael and **Beit-Hallahmi, Benjamin.** The Social Psychology of Religion. *256 pp.*

Glasner, Peter E. The Sociology of Secularisation. *A Critique of a Concept. 146 pp.*

Hall, J. R. The Ways Out. *Utopian Communal Groups in an Age of Babylon. 280 pp.*

Ranson, S., Hinings, B. and **Bryman, A.** Clergy, Ministers and Priests. *216 pp.*

Stark, Werner. The Sociology of Religion. *A Study of Christendom.*
Volume II. *Sectarian Religion. 368 pp.*
Volume III. *The Universal Church. 464 pp.*
Volume IV. *Types of Religious Man. 352 pp.*
Volume V. *Types of Religious Culture. 464 pp.*

Turner, B. S. Weber and Islam. *216 pp.*

Watt, W. Montgomery. Islam and the Integration of Society. 230 pp.

Pomian-Srzednicki, M. Religious Change in Contemporary Poland. *Sociology and Secularization. 280 pp.*

SOCIOLOGY OF ART AND LITERATURE

Jarvie, Ian C. Towards a Sociology of the Cinema. *A Comparative Essay on the Structure and Functioning of a Major Entertainment Industry. 405 pp.*

Rust, Frances S. Dance in Society. *An Analysis of the Relationships between the Social Dance and Society in England from the Middle Ages to the Present Day. 256 pp. 8 pp. of plates.*

Schücking, L. L. The Sociology of Literary Taste. *112 pp.*

Wolff, Janet. Hermeneutic Philosophy and the Sociology of Art. *150 pp.*

SOCIOLOGY OF KNOWLEDGE

Diesing, P. Patterns of Discovery in the Social Sciences. *262 pp.*

● **Douglas, J. D.** (Ed.) Understanding Everyday Life. *270 pp.*

● **Hamilton, P.** Knowledge and Social Structure. *174 pp.*

Jarvie, I. C. Concepts and Society. *232 pp.*

Mannheim, Karl. Essays on the Sociology of Knowledge. *Edited by Paul Kecskemeti. Editorial Note by Adolph Lowe. 353 pp.*

Remmling, Gunter W. The Sociology of Karl Mannheim. *With a Bibliographical Guide to the Sociology of Knowledge, Ideological Analysis, and Social Planning. 255 pp.*

Remmling, Gunter W. (Ed.) Towards the Sociology of Knowledge. *Origin and Development of a Sociological Thought Style. 463 pp.*

Scheler, M. Problems of a Sociology of Knowledge. *Trans. by M. S. Frings. Edited and with an Introduction by K. Stikkers. 232 pp.*

URBAN SOCIOLOGY

Aldridge, M. The British New Towns. *A Programme Without a Policy. 232 pp.*

Ashworth, William. The Genesis of Modern British Town Planning: *A Study in Economic and Social History of the Nineteenth and Twentieth Centuries. 288 pp.*

Brittan, A. The Privatised World. *196 pp.*

Cullingworth, J. B. Housing Needs and Planning Policy: *a Restatement of the Problems of Housing Need and 'Overspill' in England and Wales. 232 pp. 44 tables. 8 maps.*

Dickinson, Robert E. City and Region: *A Geographical Interpretation. 608 pp. 125 figures.*
The West European City: *A Geographical Interpretation. 600 pp. 129 maps. 29 plates.*

Humphreys, Alexander J. New Dubliners: *Urbanization and the Irish Family.*
Foreword by George C. Homans. 304 pp.

Jackson, Brian. Working Class Community: *Some General Notions raised by a*
Series of Studies in Northern England. 192 pp.

● Mann, P. H. An Approach to Urban Sociology. *240 pp.*

Mellor, J. R. Urban Sociology in an Urbanized Society. *326 pp.*

Morris, R. N. and Mogey, J. The Sociology of Housing. *Studies at Berinsfield.*
232 pp. 4 pp. plates.

Mullan, R. Stevenage Ltd. *438 pp.*

Rex, J. and Tomlinson, S. Colonial Immigrants in a British City. *A Class*
Analysis. 368 pp.

Rosser, C. and Harris, C. The Family and Social Change. *A Study of Family*
and Kinship in a South Wales Town. 352 pp. 8 maps.

● Stacey, Margaret, Batsone, Eric, Bell, Colin and Thurcott, Anne. Power,
Persistence and Change. *A Second Study of Banbury. 196 pp.*

RURAL SOCIOLOGY

● Mayer, Adrian C. Peasants in the Pacific. *A Study of Fiji Indian Rural Society.*
248 pp. 20 plates.

Williams, W. M. The Sociology of an English Village: *Gosforth. 272 pp.*
12 figures. 13 tables.

SOCIOLOGY OF INDUSTRY AND DISTRIBUTION

Dunkerley, David. The Foreman. *Aspects of Task and Structure. 192 pp.*

Eldridge, J. E. T. *Industrial Disputes. Essays in the Sociology of Industrial*
Relations. 288 pp.

Hollowell, Peter G. The Lorry Driver. *272 pp.*

● Oxaal, I., Barnett, T. and Booth, D. (Eds) Beyond the Sociology of
Development. *Economy and Society in Latin America and Africa. 295 pp.*

Smelser, Neil J. Social Change in the Industrial Revolution: *An Application of*
Theory to the Lancashire Cotton Industry, 1770–1840. 468 pp. 12 figures.
14 tables.

Watson, T. J. The Personnel Managers. *A Study in the Sociology of Work and*
Employment, 262 pp.

ANTHROPOLOGY

Brandel-Syrier, Mia. Reeftown Elite. *A Study of Social Mobility in a Modern*
African Community on the Reef. 376 pp.

Dickie-Clark, H. F. The Marginal Situation. *A Sociological Study of a Coloured*
Group. 236 pp.

Dube, S. C. Indian Village. *Foreword by Morris Edward Opler. 276 pp.*
4 plates.

India's Changing Villages: *Human Factors in Community Development.*
260 pp. 8 plates. 1 map.

Fei, H.-T. Peasant Life in China. *A Field Study of Country Life in the Yangtze*
Valley. With a foreword by Bronislaw Malinowski. 328 pp. 16 pp. plates.

Firth, Raymond. Malay Fishermen. *Their Peasant Economy. 420 pp. 17 pp.*
plates.

Gulliver, P. H. Social Control in an African Society: a Study of the Arusha,
Agricultural Masai of Northern Tanganykia. *320 pp. 8 plates. 10 figures.*
Family Herds. *288 pp.*

Jarvie, Ian C. The Revolution in Anthropology. *268 pp.*

Little, Kenneth L. Mende of Sierra Leone. *308 pp. and folder.*

Negroes in Britain. *With a New Introduction and Contemporary Study by*
Leonard Bloom. 320 pp.

9

Tambs-Lyche, H. London Patidars. *168 pp.*
Madan, G. R. Western Sociologists on Indian Society. *Marx, Spencer, Weber, Durkheim, Pareto. 384 pp.*
Mayer, A. C. Peasants in the Pacific. *A Study of Fiji Indian Rural Society. 248 pp.*
Meer, Fatima. Race and Suicide in South Africa. *325 pp.*
Smith, Raymond T. The Negro Family in British Guiana: *Family Structure and Social Status in the Villages. With a Foreword by Meyer Fortes. 314 pp. 8 plates. 1 figure. 4 maps.*

SOCIOLOGY AND PHILOSOPHY

● Adriaansens, H. Talcott Parsons and the Conceptual Dilemma. *200 pp.*
Barnsley, John H. The Social Reality of Ethics. *A Comparative Analysis of Moral Codes. 448 pp.*
Diesing, Paul. Patterns of Discovery in the Social Sciences. *362 pp.*
● Douglas, Jack D. (Ed.) Understanding Everyday Life. *Toward the Reconstruction of Sociological Knowledge. Contributions by Alan F. Blum, Aaron W. Cicourel, Norman K. Denzin, Jack D. Douglas, John Heeren, Peter McHugh, Peter K. Manning, Melvin Power, Matthew Speier, Roy Turner, D. Lawrence Wieder, Thomas P. Wilson and Don H. Zimmerman. 370 pp.*
Gorman, Robert A. The Dual Vision. *Alfred Schutz and the Myth of Phenomenological Social Science. 240 pp.*
Jarvie, Ian C. Concepts and Society. *216 pp.*
Kilminster, R. Praxis and Method. *A Sociological Dialogue with Lukács, Gramsci and the Early Frankfurt School. 334 pp.*
Outhwaite, W. Concept Formation in Social Science. *255 pp.*
● Pelz, Werner. The Scope of Understanding in Sociology. *Towards a More Radical Reorientation in the Social Humanistic Sciences. 283 pp.*
Roche, Maurice, Phenomenology, Language and the Social Sciences. *371 pp.*
Sahay, Arun. Sociological Analysis. *212 pp.*
● Slater, P. Origin and Significance of the Frankfurt School. *A Marxist Perspective. 185 pp.*
Spurling, L. Phenomenology and the Social World. *The Philosophy of Merleau-Ponty and its Relation to the Social Sciences. 222 pp.*
Wilson, H. T. The American Ideology. *Science, Technology and Organization as Modes of Rationality. 368 pp.*

International Library of Anthropology
General Editor Adam Kuper

● Ahmed, A. S. Millennium and Charisma Among Pathans. *A Critical Essay in Social Anthropology. 192 pp.*
Pukhtun Economy and Society. *Traditional Structure and Economic Development. 422 pp.*
Barth, F. Selected Essays. *Volume 1. 256 pp.* Selected Essays. *Volume II. 200 pp.*
Brown, Paula. The Chimbu. *A Study of Change in the New Guinea Highlands. 151 pp.*
Duller, H. J. Development Technology. *192 pp.*
Foner, N. Jamaica Farewell. *200 pp.*
Gudeman, Stephen. Relationships, Residence and the Individual. *A Rural Panamanian Community. 288 pp. 11 plates, 5 figures, 2 maps, 10 tables.*
The Demise of a Rural Economy. *From Subsistence to Capitalism in a Latin American Village. 160 pp.*

10

Hamnett, Ian. Chieftainship and Legitimacy. *An Anthropological Study of Executive Law in Lesotho. 163 pp.*
Hanson, F. Allan. Meaning in Culture. *127 pp.*
Hazan, H. The Limbo People. *A Study of the Constitution of the Time Universe Among the Aged. 208 pp.*
Humphreys, S. C. Anthropology and the Greeks. *288 pp.*
Karp, I. Fields of Change Among the Iteso of Kenya. *140 pp.*
Kuper, A. Wives for Cattle. *Bridewealth in Southern Africa. 224 pp.*
Lloyd, P. C. Power and Independence. *Urban Africans' Perception of Social Inequality. 264 pp.*
Malinowski, B. and de la Fuente, J. Malinowski in Mexico. *The Economics of a Mexican Market System. Edited and Introduced by Susan Drucker-Brown. About 240 pp.*
Parry, J. P. Caste and Kinship in Kangra. *352 pp. Illustrated.*
Pettigrew, Joyce. Robber Noblemen. *A Study of the Political System of the Sikh Jats. 284 pp.*
Street, Brian V. The Savage in Literature. *Representations of 'Primitive' Society in English Fiction, 1858–1920. 207 pp.*
Van Den Berghe, Pierre L. Power and Privilege at an African University. *278 pp.*

International Library of Phenomenology and Moral Sciences
General Editor John O'Neill

Adorno, T. W. Aesthetic Theory. Translated by C. Lenhardt.
Apel, K.-O. Towards a Transformation of Philosophy. *308 pp.*
Bologh, R. W. Dialectical Phenomenology. *Marx's Method. 287 pp.*
Fekete, J. The Critical Twilight. *Explorations in the Ideology of Anglo-American Literary Theory from Eliot to McLuhan. 300 pp.*
Green, B. S. Knowing the Poor. *A Case Study in Textual Reality Construction. 200 pp.*
McHoul, A. W. How Texts Talk. *Essays on Reading and Ethnomethodology. 163 pp.*
Medina, A. Reflection, Time and the Novel. *Towards a Communicative Theory of Literature. 143 pp.*
O'Neill, J. Essaying Montaigne. *A Study of the Renaissance Institution of Writing and Reading. 244 pp.*
Schutz. A. Life Forms and Meaning Structure. *Translated, Introduced and Annotated by Helmut Wagner. 207 pp.*

International Library of Social Policy
General Editor Kathleen Jones

Bayley, M. Mental Handicap and Community Care. *426 pp.*
Bottoms, A. E. and McClean, J. D. Defendants in the Criminal Process. *284 pp.*
Bradshaw, J. The Family Fund. *An Initiative in Social Policy. 248 pp.*
Butler, J. R. Family Doctors and Public Policy. *208 pp.*
Davies, Martin. Prisoners of Society. *Attitudes and Aftercare. 204 pp.*
Gittus, Elizabeth. Flats, Families and the Under-Fives. *285 pp.*
Holman, Robert. Trading in Children. *A Study of Private Fostering. 355 pp.*
Jeffs, A. Young People and the Youth Service. *160 pp.*
Jones, Howard and Cornes, Paul. Open Prisons. *288 pp.*
Jones, Kathleen. History of the Mental Health Service. *428 pp.*

Jones, Kathleen with Brown, John, Cunningham, W. J., Roberts, Julian and
   Williams, Peter. Opening the Door. *A Study of New Policies for the
   Mentally Handicapped. 278 pp.*
Karn, Valerie. Retiring to the Seaside. *400 pp. 2 maps. Numerous tables.*
King, R. D. and Elliot, K. W. Albany: Birth of a Prison—End of an Era.
   294 pp.
Thomas, J. E. The English Prison Officer since 1850. *258 pp.*
Walton, R. G. Women in Social Work. *303 pp.*
● Woodward, J. To Do the Sick No Harm. *A Study of the British Voluntary
   Hospital System to 1875. 234 pp.*

International Library of Welfare and Philosophy
General Editors Noel Timms and David Watson

○ Campbell, J. The Left and Rights. *A Conceptual Analysis of the Idea of
   Socialist Rights. About 296 pp.*
● McDermott, F. E. (Ed.) Self-Determination in Social Work. *A Collection of
   Essays on Self-determination and Related Concepts by Philosophers and
   Social Work Theorists. Contributors: F. P. Biestek, S. Bernstein, A. Keith-
   Lucas, D. Sayer, H. H. Perelman, C. Whittington, R. F. Stalley, F. E.
   McDermott, I. Berlin, H. J. McCloskey, H. L. A. Hart, J. Wilson, A. I.
   Melden, S. I. Benn. 254 pp.*
● Plant, Raymond. Community and Ideology. *104 pp.*
● Plant, Raymond, Lesser, Harry and Taylor-Gooby, Peter. Political Philosophy
   and Social Welfare. *Essays on the Normative Basis of Welfare Provision.
   276 pp.*
Ragg, N. M. People Not Cases. *A Philosophical Approach to Social Work.
   168 pp.*
Timms, Noel (Ed.) Social Welfare. *Why and How? 316 pp. 7 figures.*
● Timms, Noel and Watson, David (Eds) Talking About Welfare. *Readings in
   Philosophy and Social Policy. Contributors: T. H. Marshall, R. B. Brandt,
   G. H. von Wright, K. Nielsen, M. Cranston, R. M. Titmuss, R. S. Downie,
   E. Telfer, D. Donnison, J. Benson, P. Leonard. A. Keith-Lucas, D. Walsh,
   I. T. Ramsey. 230 pp.*
● Philosophy in Social Work. *250 pp.*
● Weale, A. Equality and Social Policy. *164 pp.*

Library of Social Work
General Editor Noel Timms

● Baldock, Peter. Community Work and Social Work. *140 pp.*
○ Beedell, Christopher. Residential Life with Children. *210 pp. Crown 8vo.*
● Berry, Juliet. Daily Experience in Residential Life. *A Study of Children and
   their Care-givers. 202 pp.*
○ Social Work with Children. *190 pp. Crown 8vo.*
● Brearley, C. Paul. Residential Work with the Elderly. *116 pp.*
● Social Work, Ageing and Society. *126 pp.*
● Cheetham, Juliet. Social Work with Immigrants. *240 pp. Crown 8vo.*
● Cross, Crispin P. (Ed.) Interviewing and Communication in Social Work.
   *Contributions by C. P. Cross, D. Laurenson, B. Strutt, S. Raven. 192 pp.
   Crown 8vo.*
● Curnock, Kathleen and Hardiker, Pauline. Towards Practice Theory. *Skills and
   Methods in Social Assessments. 208 pp.*
● Davies, Bernard. The Use of Groups in Social Work Practice. *158 pp.*
Davies, Bleddyn and Knapp, M. Old People's Homes and the Production of
   Welfare. *264 pp.*

● **Davies, Martin.** Support Systems in Social Work. *144 pp.*

Ellis, June. (Ed.) West African Families in Britain. *A Meeting of Two Cultures. Contributions by Pat Stapleton, Vivien Biggs. 150 pp. 1 map.*

○ **Ford, J.** Human Behaviour. *Towards a Practical Understanding. About 160 pp.*

● **Hart, John.** Social Work and Sexual Conduct. *230 pp.*

Heraud, Brian. Training for Uncertainty. *A Sociological Approach to Social Work Education. 138 pp.*

Holder, D. and **Wardle, M.** Teamwork and the Development of a Unitary Approach. *212 pp.*

● **Hutten, Joan M.** Short-Term Contracts in Social Work. *Contributions by Stella M. Hall, Elsie Osborne, Mannie Sher, Eva Sternberg, Elizabeth Tuters. 134 pp.*

Jackson, Michael P. and **Valencia, B. Michael.** Financial Aid Through Social Work. *140 pp.*

● **Jones, Howard.** The Residential Community. *A Setting for Social Work. 150 pp.*

● (Ed.) Towards a New Social Work. *Contributions by Howard Jones, D. A. Fowler, J. R. Cypher, R. G. Walton, Geoffrey Mungham, Philip Priestley, Ian Shaw, M. Bartley, R. Deacon, Irwin Epstein, Geoffrey Pearson. 184 pp.*

Jones, Ray and **Pritchard, Colin.** (Eds) Social Work With Adolescents. *Contributions by Ray Jones, Colin Pritchard, Jack Dunham, Florence Rossetti, Andrew Kerslake, John Burns, William Gregory, Graham Templeman, Kenneth E. Reid, Audrey Taylor.*

○ **Jordon, William.** The Social Worker in Family Situations. *160 pp. Crown 8vo.*

● **Laycock, A. L.** Adolescents and Social Work. *128 pp. Crown 8vo.*

● **Lees, Ray.** Politics and Social Work. *128 pp. Crown 8vo.*

● Research Strategies for Social Welfare. *112 pp. Tables.*

○ **McCullough, M. K.** and **Ely, Peter J.** Social Work with Groups. *127 pp. Crown 8vo.*

● **Moffett, Jonathan.** Concepts in Casework Treatment. *128 pp. Crown 8vo.*

Parsloe, Phyllida. Juvenile Justice in Britain and the United States. *The Balance of Needs and Rights. 336 pp.*

● **Plant, Raymond.** Social and Moral Theory in Casework. *112 pp. Crown 8vo.*

Priestley, Philip, Fears, Denise and **Fuller, Roger.** Justice for Juveniles. *The 1969 Children and Young Persons Act: A Case for Reform? 128 pp.*

● **Pritchard, Colin** and **Taylor, Richard.** Social Work: Reform or Revolution? *170 pp.*

○ **Pugh, Elisabeth.** Social Work in Child Care. *128 pp. Crown 8vo.*

● **Robinson, Margaret.** Schools and Social Work. *282 pp.*

○ **Ruddock, Ralph.** Roles and Relationships. *128 pp. Crown 8vo.*

● **Sainsbury, Eric.** Social Diagnosis in Casework. *118 pp. Crown 8vo.*

● **Sainsbury, Eric, Phillips, David** and **Nixon, Stephen.** Social Work in Focus. *Clients' and Social Workers' Perceptions in Long-Term Social Work. 220 pp.*

● Social Work with Families. *Perceptions of Social Casework among Clients of a Family Service. 188pp.*

Seed, Philip. The Expansion of Social Work in Britain. *128 pp. Crown 8vo.*

● **Shaw, John.** The Self in Social Work. *124 pp.*

Smale, Gerald G. Prophecy, Behaviour and Change. *An Examination of Self-fulfilling Prophecies in Helping Relationships. 116 pp. Crown 8vo.*

Smith, Gilbert. Social Need. *Policy, Practice and Research. 155 pp.*

● Social Work and the Sociology of Organisations. *124 pp. Revised edition.*

● **Sutton, Carole.** Psychology for Social Workers and Counsellors. *An Introduction. 248 pp.*

● **Timms, Noel.** Language of Social Casework. *122 pp. Crown 8vo.*

● Recording in Social Work. *124 pp. Crown 8vo.*
● **Todd, F. Joan.** Social Work with the Mentally Subnormal. *96 pp. Crown 8vo.*
● **Walrond-Skinner, Sue.** Family Therapy. *The Treatment of Natural Systems. 172 pp.*
● **Warham, Joyce.** An Introduction to Administration for Social Workers. *Revised edition. 112 pp.*
● An Open Case. *The Organisational Context of Social Work. 172 pp.*
○ **Wittenberg, Isca Salzberger.** Psycho-Analytic Insight and Relationships. *A Kleinian Approach. 196 pp. Crown 8vo.*

Primary Socialization, Language and Education
General Editor   Basil Bernstein

Adlam, Diana S., *with the assistance of Geoffrey Turner and Lesley Lineker.* Code in Context. *272 pp.*
Bernstein, Basil. Class, Codes and Control. *3 volumes.*
● 1. *Theoretical Studies Towards a Sociology of Language. 254 pp.*
　 2. *Applied Studies Towards a Sociology of Language. 377 pp.*
● 3. *Towards a Theory of Educational Transmission. 167 pp.*
Brandis, Walter and **Henderson, Dorothy.** Social Class, Language and Communication. *288 pp.*
Cook-Gumperz, Jenny. Social Control and Socialization. *A Study of Class Differences in the Language of Maternal Control. 290 pp.*
● **Gahagan, D. M.** and **G. A.** Talk Reform. *Exploration in Language for Infant School Children. 160 pp.*
Hawkins, P. R. Social Class, the Nominal Group and Verbal Strategies. *About 220 pp.*
Robinson, W. P. and **Rakstraw, Susan D. A.** A Question of Answers. *2 volumes. 192 pp. and 180 pp.*
Turner, Geoffrey J. and **Mohan, Bernard A.** A Linguistic Description and Computer Programme for Children's Speech. *208 pp.*

Reports of the Institute of Community Studies

Baker, J. The Neighbourhood Advice Centre. *A Community Project in Camden. 320 pp.*
● **Cartwright, Ann.** Patients and their Doctors. *A Study of General Practice. 304 pp.*
Dench, Geoff. Maltese in London. *A Case-study in the Erosion of Ethnic Consciousness. 302 pp.*
Jackson, Brian and **Marsden, Dennis.** Education and the Working Class: *Some General Themes Raised by a Study of 88 Working-class Children in a Northern Industrial City. 268 pp. 2 folders.*
Madge, C. and **Willmott, P.** Inner City Poverty in Paris and London. *144 pp.*
Marris, Peter. The Experience of Higher Education. *232 pp. 27 tables.*
● Loss and Change. *192 pp.*
Marris, Peter and **Rein, Martin.** Dilemmas of Social Reform. *Poverty and Community Action in the United States. 256 pp.*
Marris, Peter and **Somerset, Anthony.** African Businessmen. *A Study of Entrepreneurship and Development in Kenya. 256 pp.*
Mills, Richard. Young Outsiders: *a Study in Alternative Communities. 216 pp.*
Runciman, W. G. Relative Deprivation and Social Justice. *A Study of Attitudes to Social Inequality in Twentieth-Century England. 352 pp.*

Willmott, Peter. Adolescent Boys in East London. *230 pp.*
Willmott, Peter and **Young, Michael.** Family and Class in a London Suburb. *202 pp. 47 tables.*
Young, Michael and **McGeeney, Patrick.** Learning Begins at Home. *A Study of a Junior School and its Parents. 128 pp.*
Young, Michael and **Willmott, Peter.** Family and Kinship in East London. *Foreword by Richard M. Titmuss. 252 pp. 39 tables.*
The Symmetrical Family. *410 pp.*

Reports of the Institute for Social Studies in Medical Care

Cartwright, Ann, Hockey, Lisbeth and **Anderson, John J.** Life Before Death. *310 pp.*
Dunnell, Karen and **Cartwright, Ann.** Medicine Takers, Prescribers and Hoarders. *190 pp.*
Farrell, C. My Mother Said. . . *A Study of the Way Young People Learned About Sex and Birth Control. 288 pp.*

Medicine, Illness and Society
General Editor W. M. Williams

Hall, David J. Social Relations & Innovation. *Changing the State of Play in Hospitals. 232 pp.*
Hall, David J. and **Stacey M.** (Eds) Beyond Separation. *234 pp.*
Robinson, David. The Process of Becoming Ill. *142 pp.*
Stacey, Margaret *et al.* Hospitals, Children and Their Families. *The Report of a Pilot Study. 202 pp.*
Stimson, G. V. and **Webb, B.** Going to See the Doctor. *The Consultation Process in General Practice. 155 pp.*

Monographs in Social Theory
General Editor Arthur Brittan

● **Barnes, B.** Scientific Knowledge and Sociological Theory. *192 pp.*
Bauman, Zygmunt. Culture as Praxis. *204 pp.*
● **Dixon, Keith.** Sociological Theory. *Pretence and Possibility. 142 pp.*
The Sociology of Belief. *Fallacy and Foundation. 144 pp.*
Goff, T. W. Marx and Mead. *Contributions to a Sociology of Knowledge. 176 pp.*
Meltzer, B. N., Petras, J. W. and **Reynolds, L. T.** Symbolic Interactionism. *Genesis, Varieties and Criticisms. 144 pp.*
● **Smith, Anthony D.** The Concept of Social Change. *A Critique of the Functionalist Theory of Social Change. 208 pp.*
● **Tudor, Andrew.** Beyond Empiricism. *Philosophy of Science in Sociology. 224 pp.*

Routledge Social Science Journals

The British Journal of Sociology. *Editor – Angus Stewart; Associate Editor – Leslie Sklair. Vol. 1, No. 1 – March 1950 and Quarterly. Roy. 8vo. All back issues available. An international journal publishing original papers in the field of sociology and related areas.*

Community Work. *Edited by David Jones and Majorie Mayo. 1973. Published
annually.*
Economy and Society. *Vol. 1, No. 1. February 1972 and Quarterly. Metric Roy.
8vo. A journal for all social scientists covering sociology, philosophy,
anthropology, economics and history. All back numbers available.*
Ethnic and Racial Studies. *Editor – John Stone. Vol. 1 – 1978. Published
quarterly.*
Religion. Journal of Religion and Religions. *Chairman of Editorial Board,
Ninian Smart. Vol. 1, No. 1, Spring 1971. A journal with an inter-
disciplinary approach to the study of the phenomena of religion. All back
numbers available.*
Sociological Review. *Chairman of Editorial Board, S. J. Eggleston. New Series.
August 1982, Vol. 30, No. 1. Published quarterly.*
Sociology of Health and Illness. *A Journal of Medical Sociology. Editor – Alan
Davies; Associate Editor – Ray Jobling. Vol. 1, Spring 1979. Published 3
times per annum.*
Year Book of Social Policy in Britain. *Edited by Kathleen Jones. 1971.
Published annually.*

Social and Psychological Aspects of Medical Practice
Editor   Trevor Silverstone

Lader, Malcolm. Psychophysiology of Mental Illness. *280 pp.*
● **Silverstone, Trevor** and **Turner, Paul.** Drug Treatment in Psychiatry. *Third
edition. 256 pp.*
Whiteley, J. S. and **Gordon, J.** Group Approaches in Psychiatry. *240 pp.*